EMERSON'S MODERNITY
AND THE EXAMPLE OF GOETHE

Emerson's Modernity
AND THE EXAMPLE OF GOETHE

Gustaaf Van Cromphout

UNIVERSITY OF MISSOURI PRESS

Columbia and London

5   4   3   2   1   94   93   92   91   90

Library of Congress Cataloging-in-Publication Data

Van Cromphout, Gustaaf.
   Emerson's modernity and the example of Goethe /
Gustaaf Van Cromphout.
      p.   cm.
   Includes bibliographical references.
   ISBN 0-8262-0734-0 (alk. paper)
   1. Emerson, Ralph Waldo, 1803–1882—Knowledge—Literature.
2. Goethe, Johann Wolfgang von, 1749–1832—Influence—Emerson.
3. American literature—German influences. 4. Modernism
(Literature)—United States. I. Title.
PS1642.L5V36   1990
814'.3—dc20   89-29235
                                                          CIP

∞™ This paper meets the minimum requirements of
the American National Standard for Permanence of Paper
for Printed Library Materials, Z39.48, 1984.

Designer: Liz Fett
Typesetter: Connell–Zeko Type & Graphics
Printer: Thomson–Shore, Inc.
Binder: Thomson–Shore, Inc.
Typeface: Sabon

To
Charles H. Foster
Vidi 'l maestro di color che sanno

CONTENTS

PREFACE

The recent ferment in Emerson studies has produced several new interpretations of his achievement. Perhaps none of these is more fascinating than the view of Emerson as our prescient contemporary, as the writer who, in Richard Poirier's words, "has already anticipated any degree of sophistication that might be brought to him" ("Human, All Too Inhuman"). Formally, critically, philosophically, Emerson now seems to have been ahead of us all along—a modernist among moderns.

The Emersonian modernity that I deal with in this book is of a different kind, however. My approach is frankly historical. I try to see Emerson in his time, as he was attempting to define his relevance to his age by creatively engaging an aggregate of attitudes and ideas that he and his contemporaries recognized as modern. Most of those attitudes and ideas Emerson and his contemporaries found expressed with unparalleled authority in the works of Goethe, the greatest writer of the age. To the nineteenth century it was Goethe who seemed to have "already anticipated any degree of sophistication that might be brought to him." To Emerson, as I shall try to show, Goethe was the quintessentially modern man, and concerned as he was with his own modernity, Emerson consequently found it impossible to avoid confronting the phenomenon of Goethe. The effect on Emerson is the subject of my book.

In presenting my evidence I have kept the German to a minimum. At times I have quoted Goethe's words for accuracy or when doing so seemed the only way of making a point tellingly. In each case, a translation or the context should make the meaning clear. All translations from Goethe are mine. I have made no attempt to turn his poetry into poetry of my own; instead, I have provided accurate prose translations. Translations of other material are also mine, unless otherwise indicated. The following list contains English equivalents of titles of major works by Goethe cited in the text:

Die Leiden des jungen Werthers	*The Sorrows of Young Werther*
Wilhelm Meisters Lehrjahre	*Wilhelm Meister's Apprenticeship*
Wilhelm Meisters Wanderjahre	*Wilhelm Meister's Travels*
Die Wahlverwandtschaften	*Elective Affinities*
Dichtung und Wahrheit	*Poetry and Truth*

Italienische Reise	*Italian Journey*
Tag-und Jahreshefte	*Daily and Yearly Journals*
Zur Farbenlehre	*Theory of Colors*
West-östlicher Divan	*West-Eastern Divan*
Winckelmann und sein Jahrhundert	*Winckelmann and His Century*

ACKNOWLEDGMENTS

I welcome this opportunity to acknowledge the debts of gratitude I have incurred in the course of writing this book. Among colleagues and friends, I owe special thanks to Arra Garab for his careful reading and detailed criticism of my manuscript; to Sean Shesgreen for much practical advice and encouragement; and to Barbara Mirel for being unfailingly on the alert for recent scholarly discussions of possible relevance to my work. My book has also benefited from the thoughtful critiques of Professor Ralph H. Orth and an anonymous reader for the University of Missouri Press.

It is also a pleasure to acknowledge two older debts. Many years ago, Professor Edwin H. Cady gave me some excellent "Occamistic" advice about scholarly writing and the marshalling of scholarly evidence that I have found advantageous ever since. Even longer ago, Charles H. Foster, to whom this book is dedicated, enlightened my mind as no one else ever did. He was my first American teacher, he introduced me to Emerson, and his teaching was so stimulating and inspiring that he made me a lifelong Emersonian. For almost three decades, moreover, he has been a true, generous friend.

I am grateful also to Glenn Meeter, who, in his dual role as departmental chairman and dear friend, has fostered an excellent academic environment and encouraged me in my scholarly endeavors for many years. Warm thanks are also due to Helen Satterlee and Karen Blaser of our College of Liberal Arts and Sciences Manuscript Services; they were invariably helpful, efficient, and patient.

Finally, I wish to express heartfelt gratitude to my wife, Luz Maria, and to our children, Beatriz and Jana Ilona, for many loving reminders that man does not live by Emerson (or even by Emerson *and* Goethe) alone.

ABBREVIATIONS

CEC   *The Correspondence of Emerson and Carlyle*. Edited by Joseph Slater. New York: Columbia University Press, 1964.

CW   *The Collected Works of Ralph Waldo Emerson*. Edited by Alfred R. Ferguson et al. 4 vols. to date. Cambridge: Harvard University Press, 1971–.

EL   *The Early Lectures of Ralph Waldo Emerson*. Edited by Stephen E. Whicher, Robert E. Spiller, and Wallace E. Williams. 3 vols. Cambridge: Harvard University Press, 1959–1972.

J   *Journals of Ralph Waldo Emerson*. Edited by Edward Waldo Emerson and Waldo Emerson Forbes. 10 vols. Boston: Houghton Mifflin Co., 1909–1914.

JMN   *The Journals and Miscellaneous Notebooks of Ralph Waldo Emerson*. Edited by William H. Gilman et al. 16 vols. Cambridge: Harvard University Press, 1960–1982.

L   *The Letters of Ralph Waldo Emerson*. Edited by Ralph L. Rusk. 6 vols. New York: Columbia University Press, 1939.

PN   *The Poetry Notebooks of Ralph Waldo Emerson*. Edited by Ralph H. Orth et al. Columbia: University of Missouri Press, 1986.

W   *The Complete Works of Ralph Waldo Emerson*. Edited by Edward Waldo Emerson. 12 vols. Boston: Houghton Mifflin Co., 1903–1904.

YES   *Young Emerson Speaks: Unpublished Discourses on Many Subjects*. Edited by Arthur Cushman McGiffert, Jr. Boston: Houghton Mifflin Co., 1938.

GA   Johann Wolfgang Goethe, *Gedenkausgabe der Werke, Briefe und Gespräche*. Edited by Ernst Beutler. 27 vols. Zurich: Artemis Verlag, 1948–1971.

When quoting from *The Journals and Miscellaneous Notebooks*, I have omitted, for the sake of easier reading, Emerson's deletions as indicated by the editors.

Emerson's Modernity
and the Example of Goethe

INTRODUCTION

EMERSON'S ACQUAINTANCE WITH GOETHE

German literature and philosophy reached their apogee during the half-century or so extending from the appearance of Goethe's *Die Leiden des jungen Werthers* (1774) and Kant's *Kritik der reinen Vernunft* (1781) to the deaths of Hegel (1831) and Goethe (1832). Though brief, Germany's moment of literary and philosophical glory profoundly affected the thought and literature of every western nation. In the United States, German literature was more influential from about 1820 to about 1850 than at any other time in our history. New England intellectuals in particular developed a keen interest in what one of them, James Freeman Clarke, called "a literature unsurpassed in the history of the world for genius, variety and extent."[1] This interest owed much to such factors as the vogue of Madame de Staël's *Germany*, which was printed in America as early as 1814, one year after its original French publication; the enthusiasm of German-educated New Englanders, including Edward Everett, George Ticknor, and George Bancroft, for the methods and achievements of German literary and historical scholarship; and the influence of such creative interpreters of German thought as Coleridge and Carlyle. Emerson remembered the early 1820s, when Everett introduced his Harvard audiences to German scholarship and criticism, as a milestone in the intellectual life of his generation (*W* 10:330, 332). Over the next two decades, German literature established itself as a major force in American culture. By 1840 the *North American Review* could report that "translations from all the distinguished authors, and imitations of every sort, already abound. A German mania prevails . . . manifest[ing] itself not only in poetry, but in various departments of literature and philosophy."[2] A year later, *The Christian Review* confirmed that German influence extended far beyond the Higher Criticism: "The general scholar, the man of taste, the classical student, the man of

1. James Freeman Clarke, "Thomas Carlyle," 422.
2. "Quarterly List of New Publications," 524.

science, the learned physician, the school teacher,—all are mastering the literature of Germany."[3]

Most widely known of all German writers was, of course, Goethe. "No author," says the first historian of New England Transcendentalism, "occupied the cultivated New England mind as much as he did."[4] The investigations of Henry A. Pochmann and of some of his precursors in the field of German-American literary relations have substantiated James Freeman Clarke's claim, in 1836, that "hardly a review or magazine appears that has not something in it about Goethe."[5] For Emerson also, "German literature" meant, above all, Goethe. During most of the 1820s Goethe was little more than a name to Emerson, but by the end of 1828 he had begun to read Goethe in German (L 1:305 n. 59). Thereafter his interest in the German writer increased rapidly, as is evident from letters and journal entries. By 1830 we find him discussing the first part of *Faust* with his brother William (L 1:305). Two years later came his introduction to Goethe's major novels—*Wilhelm Meisters Lehrjahre*, *Wilhelm Meisters Wanderjahre* (both in Carlyle's translations), and *Die Wahlverwandtschaften* (*JMN* 6:104–6, 109–11). Emerson's *vade mecum* during his Italian journey in 1833 was Goethe's *Italienische Reise*, which he read "both to practice German and for information" (*JMN* 4:178 n. 34; 137 n. 7).[6] By 1836 he had acquired what was then the most complete Goethe available, the 55–volume edition of the *Werke* published by J. G. Cotta in Stuttgart, almost every volume of which he read during the next couple of years (*JMN* 5:127 n. 390; *CEC* 269). "Nothing but the strongest conviction of Goethe's worth," Ralph L. Rusk remarks, "could have kept up the reader's courage through those discouragingly numerous little volumes of the Cotta edition" (L 1:li). But Emerson's interest extended even beyond the *Werke*, as we find him in 1837 copying passages from Goethe's letters to Schiller and to Zelter (*JMN* 5:314–16), or from Goethe's conversations as recorded by Johann Peter Eckermann in his *Gespräche mit Goethe* (*JMN* 5:290, 292, 294, 309, 313). During

3. [Barnas Sears], "German Literature;—Its Religious Character and Influence," 278.

4. Octavius Brooks Frothingham, *Transcendentalism in New England: A History*, 57.

5. Henry A. Pochmann, *German Culture in America: Philosophical and Literary Influences, 1600–1900*, 329–32, 343–47, 678 nn. 26–28; James Freeman Clarke, "Orphic Sayings. From Goethe," 60.

6. See Vivian C. Hopkins, "The Influence of Goethe on Emerson's Aesthetic Theory," 326–27.

the later 1830s, Goethe became indeed, as Rusk puts it, "almost a refrain" in Emerson's journals.[7]

Emerson was also an avid reader of material about Goethe. An early favorite was Sarah Austin's three-volume *Characteristics of Goethe: From the German of Falk, von Müller, etc.* (1833), which he began mining as early as 1834 (*JMN* 4:255; 6:113–14). Even more enthusiastic was his response to Bettina von Arnim's *Goethe's Correspondence with a Child* (1837), a mixture of fact, fiction, and wishful thinking discredited long ago (*L* 2:136; 3:77; *JMN* 7:158, 228; 8:194).[8] More valid insights into Goethe's character he derived from comments by other German contemporaries, such as those found in the *Briefe an Johann Heinrich Merck* (1835) and in Friedrich Wilhelm Riemer's *Mitteilungen über Goethe* (1841) (e.g., *JMN* 5:300; 8:279). Emerson also owed much to the most enthusiastic apostle of German literature in the English-speaking world, Thomas Carlyle. He began reading Carlyle's many essays on German subjects, several of which dealt with Goethe, as early as 1827 (*CEC* 4–7; *JMN* 5:311–12).

As his journals, letters, lectures, and essays overwhelmingly show, Emerson's reading in primary and secondary sources gave him an extensive and detailed knowledge of Goethe's works. He was as deeply interested in Goethe's scientific and critical writings as in his novels, poems, plays, and autobiographical works. References like the one to "the 150, 151 paragraphs" of the Didactic Part of the *Farbenlehre* (*L* 2:377) seem to have come to his mind as readily as details from the play *Egmont* or from the cycle of poems *West-östlicher Divan* (*JMN* 5:128, 188). No figure from post-Renaissance literature is as often quoted, as much discussed, as frequently evaluated—in short, as pervasive—in Emerson's works as Goethe.

Too much has been made of Emerson's hostile remarks about Goethe. Such remarks should be considered, first of all, in the context of the bitter controversy that marked the reception of Goethe's works in the United States as well as in Britain.[9] Most British and American intellec-

---

7. Ralph L. Rusk, *The Life of Ralph Waldo Emerson*, 207.

8. For a vigorous and persuasive early attack on the book's credibility, see George Henry Lewes, *The Life and Works of Goethe*, 510–14.

9. See Rosemary Ashton, *The German Idea: Four English Writers and the Reception of German Thought, 1800–1860*, 17–26; and Pochmann, *German Culture in America*, 330–32.

tuals, while recognizing Goethe's preeminence, were profoundly disturbed by many of his works, on grounds both moral and literary. For example, Francis Jeffrey, the famous editor of *The Edinburgh Review*, denounced *Wilhelm Meisters Lehrjahre* as "eminently absurd, puerile, incongruous, vulgar, and affected . . . almost from beginning to end, one flagrant offence against every principle of taste, and every just rule of composition . . . throughout altogether unnatural." George Bancroft, to cite another authority, concluded that "in everything that relates to firmness of principle, to love for truth itself, to humanity, to holiness, to love of freedom, [Goethe] holds perhaps the lowest place."[10] It is to Emerson's credit that he recognized that much of this hostility, his own as well as that of others, was culturally determined: "our English nature and genius has made us the worst critics of Goethe" (W 8:69). When Emerson wrote in 1832, in reference to *Wilhelm Meisters Lehrjahre*, that "the *form* of the book is for us so foreign that it long repels" (L 1:354), he revealed a sense of cultural relativity quite unlike Jeffrey's dogmatism. And when Emerson told Carlyle in 1834, referring to Goethe, that "the Puritan in me accepts no apology for bad morals in such as *he*" (CEC 107), he was making a statement not only about Goethe but also about American culture, much as T. S. Eliot did a century later when he blamed "a Calvinistic heritage, and a Puritanical temperament," among other things, for his own early antipathy to Goethe.[11] Emerson's negative comments on Goethe are usually embedded in a context of careful qualification that allows us to characterize his criticism as judicious and discerning. It is qualities such as these that give substance to Pochmann's claim that, in his Goethe chapter in *Representative Men*, Emerson "created perhaps the greatest single monument to Goethe yet produced in American criticism."[12]

It remains true, nevertheless, that Emerson was rather severe with Goethe in *Representative Men*. But this negative attitude is traceable to the philosophical positions that induced Emerson to criticize his other Representative Men with equal severity, with the exception of Montaigne, whose thoroughly self-critical skepticism made much additional criticism unnecessary. Emerson's Plato, for instance, failed as a mystic through hyperintellectualism and as a philosopher through lack of sys-

---

10. Francis Jeffrey, "German Genius and Taste: Goethe's *Wilhelm Meister*," 106; George Bancroft, *Literary and Historical Miscellanies*, 203–4.

11. T. S. Eliot, *On Poetry and Poets*, 243.

12. Pochmann, *German Culture in America*, 331.

tem. Swedenborg's achievement was marred by intellectual sterility and aesthetic insensitivity. Lacking higher seriousness, Shakespeare failed to achieve a synthesis of poetry and wisdom; the result is an oeuvre suffering from "halfness." Napoleon embodied his age's amoral pursuit of wealth and power. In such a context it is not surprising that Goethe also should have received his share of criticism. Emersonian philosophy made such criticism inevitable, on three grounds: as an idealist, Emerson was bound to regard even the most impressive incarnations of the idea, or of "the soul," as flawed and incomplete ("Our exaggeration of all fine characters arises from the fact, that we identify each in turn with the soul. But there are no such men as we fable" [*CW* 3:134]); as a Romantic quester, he was unwilling to accept the stasis and finality inherent in "perfection" ("The soul *becomes*; [and] that forever degrades the past" [*CW* 2:40]); as an apostle of self-reliance, he sought to counter excessive deference and its dangers to the self by stressing the limitations of those held up as models to humanity ("The man has never lived that can feed us ever" [*CW* 1:66]).

More important than accounting for Emerson's negative remarks, however, is that the vast majority of his statements about Goethe are positive. An examination of Emerson's total response reveals that it is predominantly informed by a deep interest, by genuine appreciation, almost by gratitude. More truly representative than any negative comment is this passage from an 1844–1845 journal:

> Putnam pleased the Boston people by railing at Goethe in his ΦBK oration because Goethe was not a New England Calvinist. If our lovers of greatness & goodness after a local type & standard could expand their scope a little they would see that a worshipper of truth and a most subtle perceiver of truth like Goethe with his impatience of all falsehood & scorn of hypocrisy was a far more useful man & incomparably more helpful ally to religion than ten thousand lukewarm churchmembers who keep all the traditions and leave a tithe of their estates to establish them. But this clergyman should have known that the movement which in America created these Unitarian dissenters of which he is one, begun in the mind of this great man he traduces; that he is precisely the individual in whom the new ideas appeared & opened to their greatest extent & with universal application, which more recently the active scholars in the different departments of Science, of State, & of the Church have carried in parcels & thimblefuls to their petty occasions. (*JMN* 9:145–46)

Emerson's journals record in voluminous detail the results of his emancipation from views like those of Putnam and Putnam's audience. What Eliot said about his own experience with Goethe is equally applicable to

Emerson's: "Antipathy overcome, when it is antipathy to any figure so great as that of Goethe, is an important liberation from a limitation of one's own mind."[13]

No recent critic has forced us to rethink the question of literary influence more radically than Harold Bloom. His redefinition of influence as revision or "correction," as a creative encounter in which a precursor's achievement is of necessity transformed, presents a far more convincing model for what actually happens when one creative personality is "influenced" by another than did the older views of influence as "receiving" or "deriving" or "borrowing." Bloom thus helps us understand, at least in a general way, the dynamics of Emerson's relationship to Goethe. Specifically, however, none of Bloom's six "revisionary ratios" seems applicable to the Emerson-Goethe relationship. For one thing, Bloom concentrates on "intra-poetic relationships"; in Emerson's encounters with Goethe, strictly poetic influences played only a secondary part. For another, Bloom presents influence as a "history of anxiety": burdened by a sense of cultural belatedness, "strong poets . . . wrestle with their strong precursors, even to the death" in order to "clear imaginative space for themselves." For several reasons, such "anxiety-as-influence" appears irrelevant to Emerson's response to Goethe. First, as a foreign writer Goethe was not a burdensome or insistent presence in any English or American writer's cultural past. Second, Emerson, to whom the present was always the best of times, was singularly immune to the anxiety of influence. However much he may have owed to precursors, he did not, as Bloom himself points out, "feel the chill of being darkened by a precursor's shadow."[14] Third, Emerson regarded Goethe, chronology notwithstanding, as representing the "future" rather than the past: for him, as for many of his contemporaries, Goethe defined and articulated a modernity that seemed ahead of its time and thus constituted a "future" beckoning to anyone concerned with his own modernity.

To Emerson, Goethe brought confidence rather than anxiety, much as, in Jonathan Bate's revision of Bloom's theory of influence, Shakespeare brought confidence to the English Romantic poets.[15] Through his achievements Goethe had proved that the modern age was not condemned to intellectual inferiority. He thus taught "courage, and the

13. Eliot, *On Poetry and Poets*, 244.
14. Harold Bloom, *The Anxiety of Influence: A Theory of Poetry*, 5, 14–16, 30, 50.
15. Jonathan Bate, *Shakespeare and the English Romantic Imagination*, 2, 5, 246–47.

equivalence of all times; that the disadvantages of any epoch exist only to the fainthearted." Far from inspiring anxiety or having a repressive effect upon his intellectual descendants, Goethe stimulated them to attempt to match his accomplishments. He was one of the "great men [who] call to us affectionately" (CW 4:156, 166). Goethe's own theory of influence supported Emerson in this interpretation of Goethe's significance.

According to Goethe, only a creative thinker or artist actively engaged in self-development can benefit from influence because only such a thinker or artist commands the energy and dynamism necessary for the assimilation of a "source." Such creative assimilation allows the source to continue as a force or impetus having a transformative effect upon the recipient's thought or art while being transformed itself by that thought or art and thus becoming, in a very real sense, the recipient's own. The entelechy (one of Goethe's terms for what is irreducibly individual in a person's development) "does not assimilate anything without contributing to it in the act of acquiring it [*ohne sich's durch eigene Zutat anzueignen*]" (GA 9:528). The source thus provokes a creative response through which a further step is achieved in a development already occurring in the recipient. When Goethe read Hafiz, for instance, he was not only deeply impressed, but, more importantly, he experienced a shock of recognition that had productive results: "Everything at all similar in matter and meaning that I had preserved and nourished in me now came into the open" (GA 11:866). Obviously, such productive responses do not result from just any encounters. To put it differently, not every source can become an influence. First of all, the thinker or artist is able to identify a potential source only as a consequence of inner development: "Merits that we know how to appreciate are embryonically present in ourselves" (GA 4:122). Second, it is the thinker's or artist's striving toward self-realization that brings an awareness of the source's active value to his further development and an ability to appropriate the source creatively. This second point is what Goethe had in mind when he said, in reference to his own indebtedness to the great minds of his age, that he had to deserve his sources by preparing himself conscientiously for his encounters with them (GA 11:860). Given the recipient's decisive role in the mediation of influence, Goethe concluded that "not only what is innately ours, but also what we are able to acquire, belongs to us and is us" (GA 9:558).

Emerson appreciated Goethe's contributive approach to influences: "It was nobly said by Goethe that he endeavored to show his gratitude to all his great contemporaries, Humboldt, Cuvier, Kant, Byron, Scott, or whosoever else, by meeting them half-way in their various efforts by the activity and performances of his own mind" (*EL* 2:125–26). Like Goethe, Emerson stressed the thinker's or artists' creative preoccupations as the basic factor in influence: "The inventor only knows how to borrow" (*CW* 4:24). Emerson also agreed that influence depends upon inner developments that bring the recipient into spiritual proximity to a source: "No man can learn what he has not preparation for learning, however near to his eyes is the object" (*CW* 2:85). To put it differently, influence occurs only if the recipient encounters a precursor "of the same turn of mind as his own, and who sees much farther on his own way than he" (*W* 7:81). Like Goethe also, Emerson insisted that what the recipient is able to acquire through influence is authentically the recipient's own. In his encounters with great literature, Emerson's thinker "is to give himself to that which draws him, because that is his own" (*JMN* 7:349). Goethe's influence, for instance, means that he often "draws out of our consciousness some familiar fact & makes it glorious by showing it in the light of thought" (*JMN* 5:225). Emerson describes this process with almost scientific accuracy when he calls Goethe "the most powerful of all mental reagents."[16] (There is, moreover, something characteristically Goethean—I am thinking especially of *Die Wahlverwandtschaften*—about Emerson's borrowing a technical term from chemistry to describe human interaction.)

Thomas McFarland recently propounded a theory of influence which, unlike Bloom's, focuses on cross-cultural relationships. Moreover, Bloom sees influence as fierce encounters between "strong" poets and their "strong" precursors, while McFarland is interested "in minimal and almost imperceptible relationships." Unlike Bloom, in other words, McFarland stresses the multiplicity of influence. Though Julie Ellison rightly claims that Bloom's readings often "take the form of a wide-ranging meditation on a multitude of earlier texts," she also recognizes that, in Bloom's view, "for the later poet . . . these [texts] tend to be felt through the work of a single writer." McFarland, on the other hand, sees more merit in Virginia Woolf's claim that "influences are infinitely numerous; writers are infinitely sensitive."[17] Each of the five forms of

16. James Freeman Clarke, Ralph Waldo Emerson, and William Henry Channing, eds., *Memoirs of Margaret Fuller Ossoli*, 1:242.

17. Thomas McFarland, *Originality & Imagination*, 35–36, 42, 49–56; Julie Ellison, *Emerson's Romantic Style*, 250 n. 9.

cross-cultural influence that he identifies reveals, however indirectly, that any significant writer is entangled in a network of multiple influences.

McFarland's impressive reminder that influence is a matter of multiple determination is likely to have a cautionary effect on anyone engaged in a study of a one-to-one relationship between two writers, the more so when the writers involved are Emerson and Goethe, to both of whom one may apply René Wellek's observation about the New England Transcendentalists: "[Their] ancestry . . . includes almost the whole intellectual history of mankind."[18] Accordingly, one must be especially wary of imprudently characterizing as "Goethean" something in Emerson that for both Emerson and Goethe is more convincingly traceable to, say, Plotinus, or Böhme, or Swedenborg. Such imprudent, and perhaps erroneous, attributions to Goethe are even more likely to occur when it might be claimed on good evidence that Emerson encountered a common precursor not directly, but *through* Goethe. My concentration on what Emerson considered Goethe's most characteristic and most pervasive trait—his modernity—has somewhat simplified my task. What Emerson recognized as truly "new," as truly "nineteenth-century" in Goethe is least likely to be some precursor's contribution disguised as Goethe's. On the other hand, the "new" might be an aspect of the *Zeitgeist* rather than something specifically Goethean. A case in point is the much-discussed Goethean doctrine of polarity. Goethe's commitment to the doctrine was constant and intense, but as McFarland has demonstrated, it was a commitment he shared with Romanticism in general.[19] Aware of such pitfalls, I have tried to be as cautious as possible in identifying what was Goethean in Emerson.

At any rate, the evidence that Goethe was a major factor in Emerson's long experiment in self-definition is overwhelming. Goethe's works Emerson considered to be "tonic books" (*JMN* 10:167), and they challenged him as no other works in modern literature did. "It is to me very plain," he wrote in 1837, "that no recent genius can work with equal effect upon mankind as Goethe, for no intelligent young man can read him without finding that his own compositions are immediately modified by his new knowledge" (*JMN* 5:314). Goethe was simply the paramount intellectual influence upon the age, the inescapable figure in modern literature. In a very real sense, his achievement defined modernity.

18. René Wellek, *Confrontations*, 164.
19. Thomas McFarland, *Romanticism and the Forms of Ruin*, 289–341.

As Emerson came to recognize, any exploration of modernity owed its significance and validity largely to the degree in which it assimilated Goethe's achievement. It is not surprising, therefore, that when in a journal entry of 1849 Emerson listed New England counterparts to his six Representative Men, he associated himself with Goethe, rather than with such old favorites as Plato, Swedenborg, and Montaigne (*JMN* 11:173).

Though immensely indebted to Goethe, Emerson remained, of course, a very different figure from the German master. Emerson put into practice his (and Goethe's) theory of influence: his relationship to Goethe's works took the form not of passive acceptance but of constructive engagement. Therefore, he interpreted, extended, transformed, and absorbed Goethean concepts and insights, and thus integrated them into his own thinking. My aim is to identify Goethe's contributions before their complete integration into Emerson's thought, that is, before Emerson's creativity made them completely Emersonian. I am not interested, in other words, in attempting the impossible task of tracing the endless mutations that Goethe's ideas underwent in the course of Emerson's development. Instead, I point to Goethe's contributions while they are still recognizable as Goethe's.

A study of the kind I have undertaken seems particularly pertinent at the present time, when our ongoing exploration of modernity has led to a renewed appreciation of the relevance of European Romantic literature. As Geoffrey Hartman noted not long ago, a major objective of contemporary criticism has been to correct "the forgetting of Romantic, and especially German Romantic, thinking" and to foster a new awareness of the modernity of that thinking. Such "forgetting" has often afflicted the study of nineteenth-century American literature. It is perhaps traceable to what Sacvan Bercovitch has called "the chronic resistance of Americanists, in their zealous search for National Character, to give due attention to 'foreign' influences." In a recent survey of research on New England Transcendentalism, Lawrence Buell rightly protested against "the excesses of contemporary scholarship, which sometimes stresses Transcendentalism's indigenous roots at the expense of its international connections."[20] Though this exceptionalist approach to American Romanticism seems to be on the wane (witness, for example, Leon

20. Geoffrey H. Hartman, *Criticism in the Wilderness: The Study of Literature Today*, 44–45; Sacvan Bercovitch, ed., *Typology and Early American Literature*, 4; Lawrence Buell, "The Transcendentalist Movement," 8.

Chai's *The Romantic Foundations of the American Renaissance* [1987]), much remains to be done.

Uncovering the roots of Emerson's modernity seems all the more important at a time when that modernity has become almost a cliché of literary history. Critics engage in endless variations upon Harold Bloom's claims that Emerson is "our father," "the American Moses," "our only inescapable [writer], to be found . . . effused and drifted all through our lives and our literature." According to Denis Donoghue, for example, Emerson is "the founding father of nearly everything we think of as American in the modern world." Or as Joseph Kronick puts it, Emerson's masterpiece, *Nature*, is "the primal source not just for New England transcendentalism but for American modernism as well."[21] The most impressive recent interpretation of Emerson's modernity is Richard Poirier's *The Renewal of Literature* (1987), which attempts to define a modern tradition that would be an alternative to modernism as it is generally understood in the twentieth century and which considers Emerson to be the source of that alternative tradition. None of these critics is primarily concerned, however, with modernity as Emerson himself understood it. As I shall try to show, that modernity is most appropriately defined as "Goethean."

The scholarship devoted so far to the Emerson-Goethe relationship falls into three categories. There is one book on the subject: Frederick B. Wahr's *Emerson and Goethe* (1915). Wahr was less concerned with Goethe's impact on Emerson than with Emerson as a critic of Goethe: "It is the aim . . . of this dissertation to treat of Emerson's critical opinion of Goethe."[22] Moreover, Wahr had no access to the mass of primary materials that have become generally available since 1915. A second book, ostensibly on Emerson and Goethe, Rüdiger Els's *Ralph Waldo Emerson und "Die Natur" in Goethes Werken* (1977), studies thoroughly though inconclusively the possible influence on Emerson's *Nature* (1836) and "Nature" (1844) of "Die Natur," a Goethean-sounding prose hymn by Georg Christoph Tobler that was mistakenly included among Goethe's works, where Emerson found it and naturally assumed it was Goethe's. Since we now know that Goethe did not write "Die Natur," I have made no use of it whatever.

---

21. Harold Bloom, *The Ringers in the Tower: Studies in Romantic Tradition*, 301–2, 305; Denis Donoghue, "Emerson at First: A Commentary on *Nature*," 45; Joseph G. Kronick, *American Poetics of History: From Emerson to the Moderns*, 1.

22. Frederick B. Wahr, *Emerson and Goethe*, 9; see also 11.

Into a second category fall the pages devoted to Emerson and Goethe in such comprehensive studies as Stanley M. Vogel's *German Literary Influences on the American Transcendentalists* (1955), Henry A. Pochmann's *German Culture in America* (1957), and Leon Chai's *The Romantic Foundations of the American Renaissance* (1987). In their treatment of specific figures, such books are of necessity limited to comments upon a few major points. Chai's impressively learned and wide-ranging study, for example, devotes only two pages to the Emerson-Goethe connection even though Goethe is an important presence in Chai's argument and Emerson is the subject of seven of his twenty-eight chapters. Similar limitations affect such long-respected general surveys as Octavius Brooks Frothingham's *Transcendentalism in New England* (1876) and Harold Clarke Goddard's *Studies in New England Transcendentalism* (1908). Both works reveal a sensitivity to the international context of Transcendentalism that is often lacking in later studies of the movement, but their panoramic intent precludes any in-depth treatment of specific Transcendentalists' responses to specific foreign sources.

A third category comprises the articles devoted to Emerson and Goethe. A large majority of these, in German as well as in English, take an approach similar to Wahr's: they examine Emerson's critical opinions or his "view" or his "image" of Goethe. Other articles, to be sure, contribute more substantially to our understanding of Goethe's significance for Emerson, and I have in my notes acknowledged, of course, any debts to them of which I am aware. Still, by their very nature, articles tend to be narrowly focused, usually exploring one aspect of Goethe's impact on Emerson in isolation from other, often complementary, aspects.

What is needed, obviously, is a study that attempts to see Emerson's relationship to Goethe in its totality. Part of such a "total" view will be the recognition that what most vitally linked Emerson and Goethe was the former's profound interest in the latter's modernity.

CHAPTER 1

GOETHE'S MODERNITY

Few words are more fluid in meaning than *modern*. The very etymology of "modern"—from Latin *modo*, "just now"—suggests both the term's perennial applicability and its consequent lack of specificity. Indeed, history shows the most varied applications of the term—from the ninth-century designation of the age of Charlemagne as *seculum modernum*, to the poetic *moderni* of the twelfth-century Renaissance, to the *via moderna* of Occam's nominalism, to the *Devotio moderna* of pre-Reformation Holland, to the Quarrel between Ancients and Moderns in the seventeenth and eighteenth centuries, and to the various modernisms of the last two centuries.[1] It is true, of course, that every generation is "modern" by virtue of its newness. But not every generation is self-consciously modern in the same degree. Not every generation considers its self-definition to depend upon a sense of tradition disrupted and of authority rejected. In every one of the historical examples cited, modernity involved thorough exploitation of a sense of discontinuity, a sense of utter difference from predecessors.

The nineteenth century was emphatic about its own modernity. The collapse of the ancien régime, the rise of Romantic self-assertion, the spread of the Industrial Revolution and its social and demographic effects, the impact of historicism and evolutionary theories all contributed to the age's sense of being a radically new epoch, an epoch witnessing the dissolution of, in Matthew Arnold's words, "the old European system of dominant ideas and facts."[2] The age also anticipated ours in claiming that in technological advances it surpassed the entire achievement of mankind before it. As Emerson put it, "our nineteenth century is the age of tools. . . . The inventions of the last fifty years counterpoise those of the fifty centuries before them" (W 7:157–58). The nineteenth-century preoccupation with Time and Becoming, moreover, resulted in a concept of modernity far more dynamic than that of any previous

1. Ernst Robert Curtius, *European Literature and the Latin Middle Ages*, 98, 254, 255 n. 23, 589; Fritz Martini, "Modern, Die Moderne," 392.
2. *The Complete Prose Works of Matthew Arnold*, 3:109–10.

period. Loyalty to the "present moment," to which the thought and literature of the age owe so much of their vitality, also precluded the attainment of stability and certitude. The old world was undoubtedly dead; but the new one, in the matrix of an ever-dissolving present, seemed indeed "powerless to be born."[3] The nineteenth century, in other words, was the first age to experience modernity as a state of perpetual crisis and as an unceasing exercise in self-definition.

Many advanced nineteenth-century thinkers considered Goethe to be the first truly modern man. A century later, such a view may seem odd. We are more likely to agree with Karl Jaspers' claim that Goethe appears to be closer to Homer than to us, or with Gottfried Benn's statement that "One hour separates Goethe from Homer; twenty-four hours separate us from Goethe, twenty-four hours of change and peril."[4] To us, Goethe seems an end rather than a beginning: the last universal genius capable of embodying a tradition stretching from the dawn of Greek civilization to his own day; the last man in history able to take all learning for his province; the last incarnation of the humanistic ideal of harmonious individual development. Our sense of the highly contingent nature of our civilization, increasing doubts about the centrality of the Western tradition, alienation and cultural fragmentation, attacks upon the very notion of a "self," and specialization—all have made an unbridgeable chasm between our world and Goethe's. Even Ernst Robert Curtius, who reacted angrily to Jaspers' casting doubt on Goethe's "adequacy" to the problems of our times, regarded Goethe's work as the final expression of a tradition beginning with Homer.[5] It seems clear that arguments about Goethe's historical situation or about his relevance to our predicament add little to our understanding of his relationship to us. Goethe *is* modern, but his modernity is of a kind that transcends time and history. Matthew Arnold illustrated the irrelevance of time to this kind of modernity when, in his lecture "On the Modern Element in Literature," he praised Thucydides as far more modern than Sir Walter Raleigh.[6] Such atemporal or ahistorical modernity is, of course, the mark of every true

3. "Stanzas from the Grande Chartreuse," line 86, in *The Poetical Works of Matthew Arnold*, 302.

4. Karl Jaspers, "Unsere Zukunft und Goethe," 125; Gottfried Benn, *Gesammelte Werke*, 4:160.

5. Ernst Robert Curtius, "Goethe oder Jaspers?"; *European Literature and the Latin Middle Ages*, 16, 587.

6. Arnold, *Complete Prose Works*, 1:25–28.

classic. Sophocles and Shakespeare are indeed our contemporaries. Having himself recognized the modernity of the *Iliad* (*GA* 9:631), Goethe has in his turn become modern in this ahistorical sense.

Many nineteenth-century thinkers, however, perceived Goethe's modernity as very much part of a historical context. Their chronological proximity to Goethe (1749–1832), if nothing else, would have prevented them from considering his achievement to be anything but a phenomenon *of* their time, *in* contemporary history. It was an achievement they regarded as constituting a radically new, a truly modern era. For example, Friedrich Schlegel, himself one of the seminal minds of the Romantic period, called Goethe "the originator of an entirely new artistic era." In one of his most famous *Fragmente*, Schlegel traced modern culture to three sources—the French Revolution, Fichte's *Wissenschaftslehre*, and Goethe's *Wilhelm Meisters Lehrjahre*, which between them had revolutionized the worlds of politics, philosophy, and literature. Though Novalis at one time considered Goethe "the true representative on earth of the poetic spirit," he later developed serious reservations about the master; but he never ceased regarding Goethe, his defects included, as utterly modern. The Norwegian Romantic philosopher Henrik Steffens, long resident in Germany, reported in his autobiography that after 1806 there was general agreement that "Goethe had created a new era." For Pushkin, *Faust* was the *Iliad* of modern life; Georg Lukács called this an excellent characterization of *Faust* but suggested one improvement: underlining the word *modern*. According to Georg Brandes, Goethe's "spirit hovers over all of modern literature: he was its prophet, and his works were its bulwark." Hippolyte Taine considered Goethe "the master of all modern minds" and regarded his *Iphigenie* as the only successful modern exemplification of the human ideal.[7]

The English-speaking world also stressed Goethe's modernity. Looking back upon his century in *Reminiscences*, Carlyle called Goethe "the first of the moderns." Much earlier, in *The French Revolution*, he had called Goethe "the spiritual counterpart" of the Revolution's "huge

---

7. Friedrich Schlegel, Letter to August Wilhelm Schlegel, 27 February 1794; Friedrich Schlegel, *Athenäum*, Fragment 216; Novalis [Friedrich von Hardenberg], *Schriften*, 2:459; 3:638–39; Henrik Steffens, quoted in Karl Robert Mandelkow, *Goethe in Deutschland*, 1:65–66; for Pushkin, see Georg Lukács, *Faust und Faustus*, 128; Georg Brandes, quoted in Fritz Strich, *Goethe und die Weltliteratur*, 351; Hippolyte Taine, quoted in *Dictionnaire biographique des auteurs*, 1:578; for Taine on *Iphigenie*, see Strich, *Goethe und die Weltliteratur*, 346.

Death-Birth of the World," a thought restated in *Past and Present*, where the French Revolution and Goethe appear as "the prophecy and dawn of a new Spiritual World." In *On Heroes, Hero-Worship and the Heroic in History*, Carlyle considered the "Hero as Man of Letters" to be "our most important modern person"; by far the greatest such modern hero was Goethe, "really a Prophecy in these most unprophetic times." The famous injunction in *Sartor Resartus*, "Close thy *Byron*; open thy *Goethe*," also suggests, of course, Goethe's special relevance to the new age.[8] Many in England shared these Carlylean views, though none of them, to be sure, equalled Carlyle's rhetoric. George Henry Lewes, for instance, whose *The Life and Works of Goethe* (1855) is the first full biography of its subject in any language, described Goethe as "the great representative poet of his day—the secretary of his age." Lewes specifically stressed the modernity of *Iphigenie*, a play which so many—Emerson among them—had dismissed as a mere imitation of Euripides. In her review of Lewes's book, George Eliot treated as commonly accepted the notion that modern Europe is Goethe's intellectual child, "living chiefly on the ideas it has inherited from him."[9]

No English writer was more insistent than Matthew Arnold in claiming that Goethe was the intellectual father of modern Europe. In his essay on Heinrich Heine, Arnold described Goethe as "absolutely fatal to all routine thinking" and hence as "really subversive of the foundations on which the old European order rested." Elsewhere Arnold put it thus: "When Goethe came, Europe had lost her basis of spiritual life; she had to find it again; Goethe's task was,—the inevitable task of the modern poet henceforth is,— . . . to interpret human life afresh, and to supply a new spiritual basis to it." Indeed, Goethe, "in the width, depth, and richness of his criticism of life, by far our greatest modern man," articulated the modern problem as no one else did and pointed to its solution; therefore, "no persons [are] so thoroughly modern, as those who have felt Goethe's influence most deeply."[10]

Emerson was in full agreement with such views. He called Goethe "the pivotal mind in modern literature,—for all before him are ancients,

8. Thomas Carlyle, *Reminiscences*, 282; *The Works of Thomas Carlyle*, 4:55; 10: 236; 5:155, 157; 1:153.

9. Lewes, *Life and Works of Goethe*, 135, 269–81; George Eliot, quoted in Ashton, *German Idea*, 134.

10. Arnold, *Complete Prose Works* 3:110, 381; 8:275.

and all who have read him are moderns."[11] When posterity examines the
nineteenth century, Emerson ventured to predict, none among "the
events of culture" will rank in importance with "the reading of Goethe."
Indeed, "Goethe was the cow from which all their milk was drawn"
(*JMN* 11:382). In view of Emerson's deep commitment to every generation's right to its own insights, no statement perhaps better reveals his
sense of Goethe's continuing modernity than this 1851 journal entry:
"No matter that you were born since Goethe died,—if you have not read
Goethe . . . you . . . belong with the antediluvians" (*JMN* 11:430). For
Emerson, Goethe was simply "the soul of his century," or to put it more
elaborately: "Of all men he who has united in himself, and that in the
most extraordinary degree, the tendencies of the era, is the German poet,
naturalist and philosopher, Goethe" (*CW* 4:157; *W* 12:322). Not surprisingly, Goethe appears the most modern by far of Emerson's Representative Men.

What exactly did nineteenth-century writers mean when they referred
to Goethe as "modern"? It goes without saying that those most vitally
affected by his example did not picture him as the serene Olympian of
critical legend. Instead they regarded him as the man who had experienced most fundamentally the problems and paradoxes constituting
modern life and as the writer whose works were a record of that experience unsurpassed in vitality and scope. When Carlyle, for instance, said
that he felt "endlessly indebted to *Goethe*," he was not referring to
Goethe's supposed Olympianism, but to his long, painful, and up to a
point successful search for solutions to the problems confronting modern man: "He, in his fashion, I perceived, had travelled the steep rocky
road before me,—the first of the moderns."[12] In his poetic "last will and
testament," the late poem "Vermächtnis," Goethe says that the most
laudable of all pursuits is "edlen Seelen vorzufühlen": to anticipate noble
souls in their search for answers intellectual or aesthetic (*GA* 1:516).
One way in which Goethe had anticipated Carlyle in particular, and the
nineteenth century in general—and, as Barker Fairley rightly stresses,
our time as well—was in his preoccupation not only with the self, but
with self-consciousness.[13] As no one before him, Goethe explored the

11. Clarke, Emerson, and Channing, eds., *Memoirs of Margaret Fuller Ossoli*, 1:242.
12. Carlyle, *Reminiscences*, 282.
13. Barker Fairley, *A Study of Goethe*, vi.

threats to the self resulting from excessive introspection and introversion. *Die Leiden des jungen Werthers* and *Torquato Tasso* gave voice to what Emerson recognized as "the age of the first person singular," an age when "the young men were born with knives in their brain, a tendency to introversion, self-dissection, anatomizing of motives" (*JMN* 3:70; *W* 10:329). As far as Emerson was concerned, Goethe was clearly the chief interpreter of this modern tendency: "The most remarkable literary work of the age has for its hero and subject precisely this introversion: I mean the poem of Faust" (*W* 10:328). More powerfully than any other work of the time, *Faust* showed that what introspection ultimately discovered was scission, a self divided against itself. For Emerson, the essence of *Faust* manifested itself in the protagonist's famous lament: "Zwei Seelen wohnen, ach! in meiner Brust, / Die eine will sich von der andern trennen" (Two souls, alas, reside within my breast, and either would be severed from the other; *GA* 5:177, lines 1112–13). As Joel Porte has remarked, Emerson recognized "that in drawing the portrait of a radically divided soul, Goethe had created the central imaginative document of his time."[14]

Like many of his contemporaries, Goethe contrasted modern fragmentation with the presumed wholeness of man in antiquity, when "feeling and reflection were not yet fragmented, [when] that hardly curable dissociation in healthy human nature had not yet occurred" (*GA* 13:418). The truly unique achievement, Goethe said in *Winckelmann und sein Jahrhundert*, results from the harmonious integration of man's total powers. Such integration was "the fortunate destiny of the ancients, especially of the Greeks in their greatest epoch"; the moderns, by contrast, are fated to embody division (*GA* 13:416–17). Goethe further elaborated this distinction in his essay "Shakespeare und kein Ende." Whereas the ancients were "naive" (in Schiller's sense of the term: at one with and expressing nature), the moderns are "sentimental" (in Schiller's sense: trying to reestablish contact with nature); whereas the ancients embodied "reality," the moderns, divorced from "reality," try to recapture it through pursuit of the "ideal"; whereas ancient literature expressed "necessity" and "obligation," modern literature expresses "freedom" and "the will." In short, whereas the ancients were classical, the moderns are romantic (*GA* 14:760). Schiller, as is well known, classified Goethe as a "naive" poet born in a "sentimental" age.[15] What Goethe

14. Joel Porte, "Emerson, Thoreau, and the Double Consciousness," 41.
15. Friedrich Schiller, *Über naive und sentimentalische Dichtung*, in *Werke*, 4:287–

derived above all, however, from Schiller's speculations was a deeper sense of his own modernity. As he told Karl Friedrich von Reinhard, Schiller's *Über naive und sentimentalische Dichtung* made him realize that the age and his own development had made him part of modern poetry (*GA* 22:465). "[Schiller] proved to me," Goethe told Eckermann in later years, "that I was a romantic in spite of myself, and that because of the predominance of sentiment [even] my *Iphigenie* was by no means so classical or so ancient in spirit as one might have supposed" (*GA* 24:405–6). In fact, Goethe told Eckermann in another context in which he contrasted ancient wholeness with modern incompleteness, "I was unable to deny my modernity" (*GA* 24:65). Goethe's "modern" achievement was such that, in René Wellek's words, "he, as much as any single writer, helped to create . . . the European romantic movement."[16] If romanticism was sickly, as Goethe once said (*GA* 24:332), his literary career also provided the nineteenth century with its most impressive example of sickness overcome. Hence his reputation, from Carlyle to T. S. Eliot, as "Teacher" and "Sage," or, in Matthew Arnold's insistently medical formulation, as "Physician of the Iron Age":

> He took the suffering human race,
> He read each wound, each weakness clear;
> And struck his finger on the place,
> And said: *Thou ailest here, and here.*[17]

A second way in which Goethe demonstrated his modernity was in his attitude toward culture. By the later eighteenth century, as Hegel argued in his *Phänomenologie des Geistes* (1807), culture had become a source of alienation, a factor antithetical to the self in the dialectic of self-realization. As antithesis, culture was both necessary and negative. Hence it became increasingly a "problem" to be analyzed and interpreted, and a force to be criticized and resisted. The individual, once organically a part of the culture, now confronted it. "The modern period," Lionel Trilling concurs, "had its beginning in the latter part of the eighteenth century" because then arose the belief "that a primary function of art and thought is to liberate the individual from the tyranny of his culture in the environmental sense and to permit him to stand

368; see also Schiller's important letter to Goethe, 23 August 1794 (*GA* 20:13–16).

16. René Wellek, *Concepts of Criticism*, 163.

17. Arnold, "Memorial Verses," lines 19–22, in *Poetical Works*, 270.

beyond it in an autonomy of perception and judgment."[18] To the nine-teenth century Goethe was the chief liberator in the sense suggested by Trilling. Goethe himself had claimed as much: he considered himself the liberator of the new generation because he had taught them that the final criterion of life and art was man's individuality (GA 14:398). In Arnold's words, Goethe's "most important line of activity" was his "liberation of the modern European from the old routine"; he accomplished this liber-ation by putting "the standard, once for all, inside every man instead of outside him."[19] Similarly, Emerson's Goethe, "coming into an over-civilized time and country, when original talent was oppressed under the load of books and mechanical auxiliaries . . . taught men how to dispose of this mountainous miscellany, and make it subservient" (CW 4:166). Drawing his strength "from nature with which he lived in full commu-nion," Goethe was able to pierce "the variety of coats of convention with which life had got encrusted" (CW 4:156). In sum, he represents "the impatience and reaction of nature against the *morgue* of conventions" (CW 4:166).

As representative of "nature," Goethe not only disposed of the old and conventional but gave voice to the aspirations and aims of the nineteenth century (CW 4:156). The new age, as Hegel emphasized in one of his remarkable analyses of the modern condition, was so prosaic and com-plex that it made heroism impossible; its tone was bourgeois and demo-cratic rather than heroic or aristocratic.[20] Emerson stressed that Goethe had expressed more successfully than anyone else the values and aspira-tions of an age marked by "the absence of heroic characters" (CW 4:156)—a view of Goethe supported in our time by, among others, Thomas Mann and Georg Lukács.[21] Emerson quotes with approval Novalis's characterization of *Wilhelm Meisters Lehrjahre* as a book "thoroughly modern and prosaic," which "treats only of the ordinary affairs of men" and is "a poeticized civic and domestic story" (CW

18. Georg Wilhelm Friedrich Hegel, *Phänomenologie des Geistes*, 350–76; Lionel Trilling, *Beyond Culture*, xiii.

19. Arnold, *Complete Prose Works*, 3:108, 110.

20. Georg Wilhelm Friedrich Hegel, *Vorlesungen über die Aesthetik*, in *Sämtliche Werke*, 12:245–68. See also Georg Lukács, *The Historical Novel*, 30–63; and Mario Praz, *The Hero in Eclipse in Victorian Fiction*.

21. Thomas Mann, "Goethe als Repräsentant des bürgerlichen Zeitalters" and "Goe-the und die Demokratie," in *Gesammelte Werke* 9:297–332, 755–82; Lukács, *Faust und Faustus*, 30–46.

4:161).[22] Poeticizing "the common . . . the familiar, the low" was the function of the writer of the new age, Emerson maintained in *The American Scholar*; and Goethe was "the most modern of the moderns" precisely because of his "perception of the worth of the vulgar" (*CW* 1:67–68). By "democratizing" literature in both content and form, Goethe was able to "clothe . . . our modern existence with poetry" (*CW* 4:157).

The nineteenth century also considered Goethe utterly modern in his lifelong preoccupation with and exemplification of development and metamorphosis. Not only did he perceive unremitting change and process in nature (in science, as is well known, he was implacable in his hostility to all static and mechanistic views), but he also experienced them as his mode of existence, as the vehicles of what Emil Staiger has called his "ewige Werdelust," his "never-ending passion for becoming."[23] His chameleonic tendency, which Goethe and those who knew him personally considered a fundamental trait of his character, found expression in the highly tentative nature of many of his literary experiments, quite a number of which remained fragments, while others (e.g., *Faust*) went through years or even decades of rethinking before reaching completion.[24] An apt motto for Goethe's literary career—always breaking new ground, dynamic, open-ended, protean, impossible to encapsulate—is found in a striking dialogue from *Faust, Part Two*:

> Wohin der Weg?
>   Kein Weg! Ins Unbetretene . . .
>   (*GA* 5:338, line 6222)
>
> (Where is the path?
>   There is no path! Into the untrodden . . .)

It seems inconceivable, after all, that the novelist of *Die Leiden des jungen Werthers* should also have written *Wilhelm Meisters Wanderjahre*; or that the same poet should have written "Nur wer die Sehnsucht kennt" and the *Römische Elegien*; or the same playwright *Götz von Berlichingen* and *Iphigenie auf Tauris*; or that the author of any of the above should have written *Die Metamorphose der Pflanzen* and the *Farbenlehre*. As Emerson saw it, this very variety was itself an expression

22. Novalis, *Schriften*, 3:638–39; see also 2:640; 3:326, 646–47.
23. Emil Staiger, *Goethe*, 1:524.
24. Fairley, *Study of Goethe*, 4–26.

of Goethe's modernity. Whereas ancient or medieval life, in Emerson's cultural typology, was "a simple and comprehensible affair," modern life was utterly distracting in its multiplicity, a "rolling miscellany of facts and sciences." Through his versatility, Goethe, "hundred-handed, Argus-eyed," could become "the philosopher of this multiplicity" and "dispose of [it] with ease" (CW 4:156). As already hinted, Goethe's versatility is stylistic as well as conceptual. It is characteristic of Goethe, Georg Lukács has said, that "stylistically he hardly ever repeats himself." Each of his major works "has its own peculiar . . . organically developed style." What most of his styles do have in common is movement itself: Goethe's lines surge and sweep and rush and throb, or more quietly, they flow or evolve. Friedrich Gundolf has highlighted this quality in his careful examination of the verbal devices in Goethe's poetry, which in E. M. Butler's words, "is more dynamic than that of any other poet in the world."[25]

On the psychological level, the preoccupation with movement takes the form of will and striving. Goethe anticipated much of nineteenth-century thought when he called the will "the God of the modern age" (GA 14:762). More specifically, "a will that reaches beyond a man's powers is modern" (GA 14:763). Such striving is, of course, the leitmotiv of Faust (e.g., lines 317, 1075, 1676, 1742, 7291; GA 5:151, 176, 193, 195, 373). It is also Faust's road to salvation. He is granted redemption precisely because he has striven without cease, as the angels make emphatically clear near the end of Faust, Part Two: "Wer immer strebend sich bemüht, / Den können wir erlösen!" (Who exerts himself in cease-less striving, to him we are permitted to grant redemption!; GA 5:520, lines 11936–37). To Goethe and to his nineteenth-century readers, Faust's most admirable trait was his infinite aspiration, his refusal to say to any moment: "Verweile doch! du bist so schön!" (Linger a while! You are so fair!; GA 5:194, line 1700).

Goethe's creative and critical explorations of these three areas—self-consciousness, the individual's ambivalent relationship to his culture, and process as the basic modality of existence—made him paradig-matically modern in the opinion of many nineteenth-century writers. The deeper their interest in Goethe, the richer and more complex indi-vidual writers' sense of his modernity became. Many discovered in

25. Lukács, *Faust und Faustus*, 204; Friedrich Gundolf, *Goethe*, 100–106; E. M. Butler, *The Tyranny of Greece over Germany*, 69.

Goethe aspects of modernity not fully accounted for by the general modern traits already indicated. Emerson considered Goethe "the great German master who towered over all his contemporaries in the first thirty years of this century" (*W* 7:237); as such, Goethe, in Emerson's view, addressed himself in his uniquely modern way to almost every question important to nineteenth-century Man Thinking.

CHAPTER 2

NATURE

When Emerson resigned from the ministry in 1832, he was aware that his reasons for doing so went beyond purely doctrinal disagreements with his congregation. His religious doubts and his resignation were his mode of experiencing and expressing a larger cultural crisis involving, as so often in history, a confrontation between "old" and "new." He complained that his ministerial role and obligations perpetuated "dead forms" and that "the profession [of minister] is antiquated" (*JMN* 4:27). In Arthur McGiffert's words, Emerson's abandonment of the ministry was "his vote in favor of the new age" (*YES* 240). Having turned his back upon the past, Emerson, at the age of twenty-nine, found himself compelled to define his role in the new world that was all before him.

Ironically, the first such definition resulted from Emerson's exploration of the old world of Europe. While in Paris in 1833, he visited the Muséum d'Histoire naturelle, where he experienced "strange sympathies" with nature and resolved to become "a naturalist" (*JMN* 4:200). Upon his return home he had lost none of his ambition of becoming a natural scientist. Beginning his career as a lyceum lecturer, he devoted his first four lectures to science; and in his first lecture, "The Uses of Natural History" (5 November 1833), he restated his intention of becoming "a naturalist" (*EL* 1:10). Soon after, however, he experienced a change of heart. By the time he delivered his fourth lecture, "The Naturalist" (7 May 1834), we hear him voicing complaints about "the evils of Science," about the scientists' being obsessed with scientific method and losing sight of the real aim of science (*EL* 1:76, 79, 80). An earlier draft of the lecture is more explicit about the grounds for Emerson's unhappiness with science. He there complains about "Pedants who mistake Classification for Science" and who forget that "all Classification is arbitrary or only approximate to natural divisions; that all Classification is only introductory,—only temporary,—convenient for collection of facts, & awaiting the discovery of the Theory which is to supersede it" (*EL* 1:417). But while attacking the scientific methods of the day, "The Naturalist" also reveals, as David Robinson has pointed out, Emerson's

24

realization that he had neither the qualifications nor the temperament to pursue a career in science.[1]

Yet the lecture also demonstrates Emerson's dissatisfaction with the prospect of being a mere "poet." As he saw it, the poet "loses himself in imaginations and for want of accuracy is a mere fabulist; his instincts unmake themselves and are tedious words" (*EL* 1:79). What Emerson advocated was a fusion of poetry and science that would make the former more "scientific" and the latter more "poetic." He claimed that he "fully believe[d] in both, in the poetry and in the dissection" (*EL* 1:79). This faith in the reciprocal enhancement of poetry and science he continued to adhere to. More than twenty years later, in the lecture "Works and Days" (first delivered in 1857), he showed that he had lost none of his conviction on this subject: "We do not listen with the best regard to the verses of a man who is only a poet, nor to his problems if he is only an algebraist; but if a man is at once acquainted with the geometric foundations of things and with their festal splendor, his poetry is exact and his arithmetic musical" (*W* 7:179). Emerson's refusal to abandon the scientific approach altogether is traceable to his realization that being a *modern* thinker or poet involved availing oneself of the insights of the scientists: "We are born in an age which to its immense inheritance of natural knowledge has added great discoveries of its own. We should not be citizens of our own time, not faithful to our trust, if we neglected to avail ourselves of their light" (*EL* 1:83). Although, as already indicated, he had no patience with mere classification of facts or objects, with all "these geologies, chemistries, astronomies [that] seem to make wise, but . . . leave us where they found us" (*W* 6:284), he never denied, as he put it in *The Conduct of Life* (1860), that "our recent culture has been in natural science" (*W* 6:218).

What Emerson demanded from science, from the beginning of his post-clerical career until the end, was a theory of nature that would provide insight into the miracle that he conceived the life of nature and of man to be. All true science, he believed, "has one aim, namely, to find a theory of nature" because "no truth can be more self evident than that the highest state of man, physical, intellectual, and moral, can only coexist with a perfect Theory of Animated Nature" (*CW* 1:8; *EL* 1:83). Unfortunately, English and American scientists failed to perceive their true mission: "Science in England, in America, is jealous of theory"; or, put differently, "English science puts humanity to the door . . . [and] is false by not being poetic" (*W* 6:284; 5:253).

1. David Robinson, *Apostle of Culture: Emerson as Preacher and Lecturer*, 84.

The theory of nature most impressive to Emerson was Goethe's. He emphasizes both the importance and the modernity of Goethe's views in statements like "He has said the best things about nature that ever were said" (*CW* 4:158) and "His love of Nature has seemed to give a new meaning to that word" (*W* 12:323). More specifically, Goethe

> has contributed a key to many parts of nature, through the rare turn for unity and simplicity in his mind. Thus Goethe suggested the leading idea of modern Botany, that a leaf or the eye of a leaf is the unit of botany, and that every part of a plant is only a transformed leaf to meet a new condition. . . . In like manner, in osteology, he assumed that one vertebra of the spine might be considered the unit of the skeleton: the head was only the uppermost vertebra transformed. . . . In optics, again, he rejected the artificial theory of seven colours, and considered that every colour was the mixture of light and darkness in new proportions. It is really of very little consequence what topic he writes upon. He sees at every pore, and has a certain gravitation towards truth. (*CW* 4:158–59)

Goethe thus became the major force behind the revolt against the eighteenth-century mechanistic worldview. He "revolted against the science of the day, against French and English science, [and] declared war against the great name of Newton" (*W* 10:338). Goethe's revolt "became a revolution"—a revolution, as Emerson sees it, that made possible not only the *Naturphilosophie* of Schelling and Oken, but also Hegel's metaphysics and a new era in "literature and the general mind" (*W* 10:338).

For Emerson, the essence of Goethe's achievement as a scientist consisted in his having developed a theory of nature in which "poetry and humanity remain to us" (*CW* 4:158). He fully approved of Goethe's anti-Newtonian *Farbenlehre*: "Goethe is right in his mode of treating colors, i.e. poetically, humanly" (*JMN* 7:411). The poetic approach is necessary because nature's "open secret" (itself a Goethean phrase)[2] "is not translateable into words," is not reducible to statement (*EL* 1:78). Emerson agrees with Goethe that ultimately it is "the province of poetry rather than of prose to describe the effect upon the mind and heart of these nameless influences" (*EL* 1:72–73).[3] In Emerson's opinion Goethe was unquestionably the greatest poet-naturalist in modern times, the

2. *GA* 9:518, 570; see also Joseph Slater, "Goethe, Carlyle, and the Open Secret."
3. For Goethe, see *GA* 16:873; 17:90, 177–78; see also such poems as "Metamorphose der Tiere" (*GA* 1:519–21; 17:267–69) and "Die Metamorphose der Pflanzen" (*GA* 1:516–18; 17:90–93).

man who came closest to fulfilling the requirements for both poet and scientist stated in "The Naturalist." It is significant that the very lecture in which Emerson reveals his profound dissatisfaction with science and scientific pursuits is riddled with references to Goethe's scientific opinions. At the very moment that Emerson abandoned the pursuit of science, David Robinson has said, Goethe helped him to maintain "his commitment to natural philosophy."[4] It is entirely in Goethe's spirit that Emerson should have called his last lecture specifically devoted to science "Humanity of Science" (delivered 22 December 1836; *EL* 2:22–40); not surprisingly, it is permeated with references and allusions to, quotations from, and paraphrases of Goethe.

In considering Goethe's unique achievement to have been the fusion of poetry and science, Emerson is in accord with the best contemporary Goethe criticism, which generally rejects the notion that the mature Goethe wasted on science time that he might have spent to better purpose on poetry. For Goethe, the two were inseparable. In Barker Fairley's words, "at the very core of [Goethe's] life" lay "his concept of wholeness or of unity and . . . the belief in nature and natural process that underlies and informs it."[5] In Goethe's thought and art, nature was the source and model, the all-pervasive, all-encompassing force. As Jean Hyppolite has said, nature meant to Goethe what history meant to Hegel: it was the "category" through which he apprehended reality.[6]

Such nature-informed unity is, of course, but another name for Goethe's pantheism. Though pantheism is a very old doctrine (Schelling traced it to the Eleatics of the fifth century B.C., as did Schopenhauer)[7] its chief modern avatar was Spinoza, who, after having been the object of merciless vilification for about a century after his death (1677), came to be regarded in late eighteenth-century Europe as an ornament to human nature and to philosophy. German poets and philosophers vied with each other in heaping praise on Spinoza, and they were chiefly responsible for his nineteenth-century fame. Given the preponderance of German thought in his century, Matthew Arnold could say that Spinoza, once "the lonely precursor of German philosophy," was bound to become "in the history of modern philosophy the central point of interest."

4. Robinson, *Apostle of Culture*, 84.

5. Fairley, *Study of Goethe*, 266–67.

6. Jean Hyppolite, *Genèse et structure de la "Phénoménologie de l'esprit" de Hegel*, 235.

7. Thomas McFarland, *Coleridge and the Pantheist Tradition*, 190 n. 1.

Thomas McFarland has amply documented his claim that Spinoza "dominated not only formal philosophy but the entire intellectual presuppositions of the nineteenth-century milieu." More specifically, "as the codifier and the purifier of all previous pantheistic views, Spinoza assumes a kind of absolute historical centrality."[8] Emerson was fully aware of the reversal in Spinoza's critical fortunes. As he noted in 1868, "In my youth, Spinoza was a hobgoblin: now he is a saint" (*JMN* 16:99). Three decades earlier, in "Literary Ethics" (1838), he praised Spinoza, together with Plotinus and other "immortal bards of philosophy," for the speculative boldness that his example inspired (*CW* 1:103). In "The Over-Soul" (1841), Spinoza appears with Kant and Coleridge as one of the philosophical "teachers sacred . . . [who] speak *from within*" (*CW* 2:170). Nevertheless, Emerson's direct knowledge of Spinoza's system seems to have been slight. Spinozism reached him primarily through the age's most eminent literary exponent of pantheism, Goethe. Arnold commented aptly on Goethe's role in the diffusion of Spinozism: "Goethe is . . . the eminent representative of a whole order of minds whose admiration has made Spinoza's fame."[9]

In his early years Emerson, as might be expected, was highly critical of pantheism. In 1827 he voiced the traditional objection that "Pantheism leads to Atheism" (*JMN* 3:76). Eight years later he was still convinced that pantheism was one of those "irrecoverable error[s]" resulting from intellectual rigidity: "The truest state of mind, rested in, becomes false. . . . It is by magnifying God, that men become Pantheists; it is by piously personifying him, that they become idolaters" (*JMN* 5:38). This journal passage shows, however, that Emerson had reached an impasse in his religious thinking. If anthropomorphism through ascribing to God the attributes of personality—individuality, awareness, emotions, subjectivity—is conducive to idolatry, the only alternative seems to be a pantheistic denial of personality to God, and this is generally the position which the mature Emerson adopted. In 1834, a year before he wrote the passage just quoted, he was already feeling his way toward pantheism: "What is there of the divine in a load of bricks? What is there of the divine in a barber's shop or a privy? Much. All" (*JMN* 4:307). From *Nature* (1836) onward, Emerson seems to have been a confirmed pan-

---

8. Arnold, *Complete Prose Works*, 3:181, 159; McFarland, *Romanticism and the Forms of Ruin*, 373; McFarland, *Coleridge and the Pantheist Tradition*, 53; and for supportive evidence, 53–106.

9. Arnold, *Complete Prose Works*, 3:177.

theist. He deified man and nature by universalizing the divine. In this regard, his remarks on prayer are revealing: "It is the soliloquy of a beholding and jubilant soul. It is the spirit of God pronouncing his works good. But prayer as a means to effect a private end, is meanness and theft. It supposes dualism and not unity in nature and consciousness. As soon as the man is at one with God, he will not beg" (CW 2:44). In the chapter on "Worship" in *The Conduct of Life*, Emerson speaks of finding "the omnipresence and the almightiness in the reaction of every atom in nature" and of "God's delegating his divinity to every particle" (W 6:215, 221–22). Emerson thus interpreting universal deification as the deity's absolute, universal immanence entailed, of course, his denying personhood to God. He repeatedly emphasizes the impersonality of God (or of "the Soul"), as in the Divinity School *Address* (CW 1:82), "Circles" (CW 2:185–86), or in this passage from "The Over-Soul":

> Persons are supplementary to the primary teaching of the soul. In youth we are mad for persons. . . . But the larger experience of man discovers the identical nature appearing through them all. Persons themselves acquaint us with the impersonal. In all conversation between two persons, tacit reference is made as to a third party, to a common nature. That third party or common nature is not social; it is impersonal; is God. (CW 2:164)

Edward Waldo Emerson quotes his father as saying, "I deny personality to God because it is too little—not too much" (W 2:391; see also JMN 5:467). Of similar import is a remark of Emerson's recorded by his cousin David Greene Haskins: "When I speak of God, I prefer to say It— It." According to William James, perhaps the most authoritative voice on this subject, Emersonianism recognizes "not a deity *in concreto*, not a superhuman person, but the immanent divinity in things."[10]

Given the frequent emergence of pantheism in the history of Western thought, several factors may have promoted Emerson's interest in it: his early exposure to Plotinus's emanationism, which, though not strictly pantheistic, sufficiently resembles pantheism to have often been regarded as such;[11] the example of Coleridge's fascination with such pantheists as Giordano Bruno, Jakob Böhme, Spinoza, and Schelling, as

10. David Greene Haskins, *Ralph Waldo Emerson: His Maternal Ancestors, With Some Reminiscences of Him*, 53; William James, *The Varieties of Religious Experience*, 31–32.

11. McFarland, *Coleridge and the Pantheist Tradition*, 354 n. 32. One of Emerson's earliest mentors in philosophy, Joseph Marie de Gérando, called Neoplatonism "un système de *Panthéisme*"; see also Kenneth Walter Cameron, *Emerson the Essayist*, 1:56.

reflected, for instance, in *Biographia Literaria* (1817); "the powerful strain of pantheism in transcendental thought," as exemplified by Carlyle; and the pantheistic tendencies inherent in some aspects of the New England religious tradition.[12] Moreover, if we are to believe Tocqueville, pantheism appealed strongly to America's democratic sensibilities:

> If there is a philosophical system which teaches that all things material and immaterial, visible and invisible, which the world contains are to be considered only as the several parts of an immense Being, who alone remains eternal amidst the continual change and ceaseless transformation of all that constitutes him, we may readily infer that such a system, although it destroy the individuality of man, or rather because it destroys that individuality, will have secret charms for men living in democracies.[13]

But whatever sources of pantheism were available to Emerson, it was clearly Goethe's pantheism that impressed him most. Goethe's was a truly modern pantheism in that it was informed by a theory of nature that, as we have seen, Emerson considered the best scientific word yet spoken on nature. In fact, Emerson counted Goethe's pantheism among the supreme achievements of human culture, as is apparent from this journal entry of 1849: "Could we some day admit into our oyster heads the immense figure which these flagrant points compose when united, the hands of Phidias, the conclusion of Newton, the pantheism of Goethe, the all wise music of Shakspeare, the robust eyes of Swedenborg!" (*JMN* 11:134).

Goethe's pantheistic view of nature was all the more accessible and attractive to Emerson on account of basic similarities between their general modes of thinking. There are four such similarities, and all of them helped shape each author's attitude toward nature. To start with the most obvious and admittedly unspecific shared characteristic, both men apprehended reality poetically rather than, strictly speaking, philosophically. Goethe confessed that he had no mind for philosophy as such: "Für Philosophie im eigentlichen Sinne hatte ich kein Organ" (*GA* 16:873). The same was true of Emerson, who had no patience with the technicalities of philosophical inquiry:

> I think metaphysics a grammar to which, once read, we seldom return. . . . I want not the logic, but the power, if any, which it brings into science and literature; the man who can humanize this logic, these syllogisms, and give me

12. On Carlyle, see Walter E. Houghton, *The Victorian Frame of Mind, 1830–1870,* 132 n. 72, 207–8, 252, 314; on the New England tradition, see Perry Miller, "From Edwards to Emerson."

13. Alexis de Tocqueville, *Democracy in America,* 2:31–32.

the results. The adepts value only the pure geometry, the aërial bridge ascending from earth to heaven with arches and abutments of pure reason. I am fully contented if you tell me where are the two termini. (*W* 12:13)

Or in a more specific vein: "Dreary to me are the names & the numbers of volumes of Hegel and the Hegelians,—to me, who only want to know at the shortest the few steps, the two steps, or the one taken. . . . It needs no Encyclopaedia of volumes to tell" (*JMN* 16:117). Goethe would have sympathized with Emerson's lament. He himself had no desire to learn "the details of the Hegelian philosophy" (*GA* 23:483), and chiefly refer-ring to Hegel, he once asked Eckermann: "What on earth must En-glishmen and Frenchmen think of the language of our philosophers, when even we Germans can't understand it?" (*GA* 24:603). For Goethe, as for Emerson, the highly technical nature of philosophy made it inac-cessible and thus prevented it from being what, according to them, it should be above all: useful. Goethe considered only that thought to be true which bore fruit for him (*GA* 21:886), or expressed aphoristically, "Only what is fruitful is true" ("Was fruchtbar ist, allein ist wahr"; *GA* 1:515). Emerson stated with similar frankness what is already implicit in the passages just quoted from him: "My metaphysics are to the end of use. I wish to know the laws of this wonderful power [of thought], that I may domesticate it" (*W* 12:13-14). He repeatedly echoed the aphorism just quoted from Goethe, as when he questioned the value of Hume and Kant and Coleridge on the grounds that only "the useful is the badge of the true" (*JMN* 10:146, 151).

In their second point of similarity, both Emerson and Goethe rejected the extreme reflexivity that characterized the epistemologies of their day. As Goethe put it, "What an odd way for philosophy, especially recent philosophy, to conduct its business! To become introspective, to sound one's own mind concerning its operations, to become entirely wrapped up in oneself—in order to get to know outward reality all the better! Is this, really, the right way?" (*GA* 13:263). In one of his "Zahme Xenien," Goethe suggests that he achieved so much because he had wasted no time thinking about thinking: "Ich habe nie über das Denken gedacht" (I never devoted any thought to thinking; *GA* 2:381). Emerson was in full accord with such views:

We have invincible repugnance to introversion, to study of the eyes instead of that which the eyes see. . . . I share the belief that the natural direction of the intellectual powers is from within outward. . . . This watching of the mind, in season and out of season, to see the mechanics of the thing, is a little of the detective. The analytic process is cold and bereaving and, shall I say it? somewhat mean, as spying. (*W* 12:12–14)

Emerson compares "the man who thought & instantly turned round to see how his thoughts were made" to Saturn devouring his children (*JMN* 5:26). With Goethe he shares the conviction that the development of the mind and self-knowledge depend upon knowledge of the "other," that is, knowledge of nature, of the world. In *Nature* he quotes an interesting statement supporting this position: "every object rightly seen, unlocks a new faculty of the soul" (*CW* 1:23). His modern editors trace this statement to Coleridge (*CW* 1:250), but actually it is Goethe's: "Jeder neue Gegenstand, wohl beschaut, schließt ein neues Organ in uns auf" (*GA* 16:880).[14] Along the same lines, Goethe confesses to a lifelong suspicion of the ancient command: "Know thyself." Man, he insists, "knows himself only to the extent that he knows the world" (*GA* 16:879–80). Or in Emerson's words: "So much of nature as he is ignorant of, so much of his own mind does he not yet possess. And, in fine, the ancient precept, 'Know thyself,' and the modern precept, 'Study nature,' become at last one maxim" (*CW* 1:55).

A third congruence lies in their wariness of system. Both Goethe and Emerson showed little appreciation of the accomplishments of the great system-builders of their day, the German idealist philosophers. No matter how ambitiously conceived, a philosophic system, Goethe and Emer-

---

14. Emerson's quotation translates Goethe's statement almost verbatim while it shows hardly any resemblance to Coleridge's passage on the discoveries of scientific men that the editors have in mind (see also *JMN* 5:189 and 3:283). The passage in *Nature* containing the quotation is based on a journal entry dated 12 August 1836 (*CW* 1:272; *JMN* 5:189). On August 8, Emerson told his brother William that "the other day" he had bought fifteen volumes of Goethe's posthumously published collected works (the *Nachgelassene Werke*), and he added: "Goethe is a wonderful man. I read little else than his books lately" (*L* 2:32–33). Goethe's statement is from "Bedeutende Fördernis durch ein einziges geistreiches Wort," an essay reprinted in volume 10 of the *Nachgelassene Werke*. Since Emerson apparently acquired these volumes very early in August and at the time read "little else" than Goethe, it is quite possible for him to have discovered by August 12 a striking passage in volume 10. This is all the more likely because Emerson, then in the last stages of readying *Nature*, must have been alerted immediately to the possible relevance of volume 10, the only one among the fifteen posthumous volumes that has "nature" in its title; the title, moreover, promises a broad theoretical approach: *Zur Naturwissenschaft im Allgemeinen*. It is also possible, of course, that Emerson had earlier knowledge of Goethe's essay—either firsthand or through a secondary source—for it originally appeared in 1823 (for this date, see Johann Wolfgang Goethe, *Werke*, edited by Erich Trunz et al. [Hamburg: Christian Wegner Verlag, 1949–60], 13:569).

son believed, could never encompass the totality of being; and no matter how subtle, a philosophic system, given its inevitable systemic imperatives, could not but fail to do justice to a reality that is inexhaustibly protean. "I confess," Emerson writes, "to a little distrust of that completeness of system which metaphysicians are apt to affect. 'T is the gnat grasping the world" (*W* 12:12). A living thought, a fresh insight, Emerson observes elsewhere, "shall . . . dispose of your world-containing system, as a very little unit" (*CW* 1:108). Or as Goethe puts it, "System of nature [*Natürlich System*]—a contradiction in terms. Nature has no system; it has, it is life and continuation from an unknown center to an unknowable circumference. The study of nature is, therefore, endless" (*GA* 17:177), an experience resembling one's having to "drink up a sea" (*ein Meer auszutrinken*; *GA* 16:870). Organizing endless, inexhaustible, mysterious nature into a whole is "a task at which all systems were bound to fail" (*GA* 23:816). Even Victor Cousin's eclecticism, which tried to combine what was best in all systems, could not hide its deficiencies long. After his brief infatuation with it, Emerson concluded: "Translate, collate, distil all the systems, it steads you nothing; for truth will not be compelled, in any mechanical manner" (*CW* 1:108). As Goethe remarked rather sardonically, "Cousin . . . does not understand that though there can be eclectic philosophers, there can be no eclectic philosophy" (*GA* 23:483; see also 9:585).

The fourth similarity in outlook between Emerson and Goethe is a natural consequence of the third: wary of system, they stay clear of it in their own works. Anyone who has wandered through the spacious world of Goethe's oeuvre must have realized how hard it is to "pin him down," how protean are the choices and situations one is confronted with. Like nature itself, his work encompasses a profusion of developments and possibilities; as in nature as he saw it, so also in his work are there a wholeness and a continuity that transcend system. In Edmund G. Berry's words, "Goethe is a veritable Heraclitus of change and diversity, and yet of a basic underlying unity."[15] Emerson did not always see the unity underlying the change and diversity, as when he suggested that Goethe was too "fragmentary" to deserve to be called a true artist (*CW* 4:165). Though Goethe admitted this apparent fragmentation, he saw his work as unified through its being grounded—no matter how varied its modes— in the depth of his experience (*GA* 10:311–12). Barker Fairley has commented most perceptively upon the intellectual dimension of Goe-

15. Edmund G. Berry, *Emerson's Plutarch*, 142.

the's experience and the grounds for his failure to meet the demands of system:

> His ideas being something that grew and ripened in him rather than came logically, it was not in his power to say halt or to stop at a given moment. The ripening went on of its own accord. This is . . . one of the reasons why he never arranged his ideas in formal order but left them lying where they happened to be, trusting to the solidarity of his work and his person to provide what order was needed.[16]

The immense vitality of Goethe's work combined with this absence of system amounts to Goethe's inviting us, Leonard A. Willoughby has said, to study him the way he studied nature; that is, in such a way that "any mental image we may form of him never hardens and becomes static."[17] This is what Goethe had in mind when, toward the end of his life, he told Chancellor von Müller that whoever entered into the spirit of his works would derive from them a certain inner freedom (*GA* 23:741).

Though Emerson occasionally deplored a lack of system in others—in Plato, for example (*CW* 4:43)—he appreciated the advantages of his own similar lack. His tone was self-congratulatory rather than contrite when he said in 1839: "I need hardly say to any one acquainted with my thoughts that I have no System" (*JMN* 7:302). Like Goethe, he trusted in a higher unity transcending all apparent fragmentariness:

> He who contents himself with dotting a fragmentary curve, recording only what facts he has observed, without attempting to arrange them within one outline, follows a system also,—a system as grand as any other, though he does not interfere with its vast curves by prematurely forcing them into a circle or ellipse, but only draws that arc which he clearly sees, or perhaps at a later observation a remote curve of the same orbit, and waits for a new opportunity, well assured that these observed arcs will consist with each other. (*W* 12:11–12)

Such characteristics of their modes of thinking and of perceiving reality made it inevitable that Goethe's and Emerson's pantheism should have lacked the philosophical rigor of Spinoza's *Ethica more geometrico demonstrata*. As George Henry Lewes pointed out, Goethe's, unlike Spinoza's, "was not a geometrical, but a poetical Pantheism."[18] Nevertheless, Spinoza's *deus sive natura* informed Goethe's entire outlook. In

16. Fairley, *Study of Goethe*, 272.
17. Leonard A. Willoughby, "Unity and Continuity in Goethe," 227.
18. Lewes, *Life and Works of Goethe*, 536.

Tag-und Jahreshefte—a work so essentially Goethean and, by extension, European that Emerson called it "a book unparallelled in America" (*JMN* 4:301)—Goethe stressed as the fundamental principle of his being (*Grund meiner ganzen Existenz*) his intuition of God in nature and of nature in God (*GA* 11:853). Spinozism, he told Friedrich Heinrich Jacobi, does justice to the highest reality: it does not prove the existence of God; it recognizes that existence is God (*GA* 18:851). Goethe's essay "Studie nach Spinoza" opens with the statement that the concept of being and the concept of perfection are one and the same (*GA* 16:841). Poetically he renders *deus sive natura* as "Gott-Natur," as in the terza rima lines inspired by Schiller's skull (*GA* 1:522). In "Gott und Welt," the cycle of poems comprising the maturest expression of Goethe's weltanschauung, the poet exalts divine immanence and scorns the notion of an extramundane God (*GA* 1:509). "Nature," we learn from one of the *Maximen und Reflexionen*, "is ever Jehovah: that's what it is, what it was, and what it will be" (*GA* 9:665). Goethe's enthusiasm for Spinoza never left him. It is as obvious in his retrospective account of his development in *Dichtung und Wahrheit* as it is in letters of the 1780s; eventually he came to rank Spinoza's influence on him with Shakespeare's (*GA* 21:191). In sum, as James Boyd remarks, Goethe's "early belief in the pantheistic one-ness which pervades all nature—Spinoza's *deus sive natura*—remained a basic, guiding principle."[19]

But Goethe also made it clear that he could not adhere to the letter (*buchstäblich*) of Spinoza's writings (*GA* 10:733). In fact, he interpreted Spinoza so creatively that, by his own admission, he could no longer distinguish between what he had derived from (*herausgelesen*) and what he had read into (*hineingelesen*) the *Ethics* (*GA* 10:684). At any rate, Goethe's *Gott-Natur* turns out to be very different from Spinoza's *deus sive natura*. For Spinoza, god-or-nature is a concept to be systematically analyzed; for Goethe—who ignored Spinoza's geometrical method of demonstration, and the abstract, indeterminate content of his absolute substance and its modifications—*Gott-Natur* is a reality to be experienced with one's heart and senses. Whereas Spinoza the philosopher, to put it differently, takes a purely theoretical view of nature, Goethe the poet responds to nature sensuously. In Martin Bollacher's words, "the rigorous immanentism (*Immanenzrigorismus*) of Spinozistic philosophy dissolves with Goethe into the visible reality of nature."[20] This rein-

19. James Boyd, *Notes to Goethe's Poems*, 2:112.
20. Martin Bollacher, *Der junge Goethe und Spinoza*, 174.

terpretation of Spinoza helped Goethe to solve some of his major problems: it responded to his need to see the world of nature as divine; it enabled him to reintegrate self and nature, and thus to overcome the painful sense of separation which his own experience had told him was the fate of the self in a mechanistic universe; and through its presentation of God, the natural world, and man as ultimately one, it enabled him to regard the activities of nature as divine models for human self-realization. As Bollacher has so aptly put it, Goethe "invests nature, as the locus of human self-realization, with the sacral attributes of divine perfection."[21]

Goethe's pantheistic universe was thus far more "natural" than Spinoza's, hence far more dynamic and creative. In large part because Goethe's universe was a living organism, René Wellek has concluded that Goethe "perfectly fits into the European romantic movement," all German debates about *Klassik* versus *Romantik* notwithstanding. For the Romantics in general, after all, the world became, as Hans Eichner has reminded us, "a great organism . . . not external to God, but in some unfathomable way identical with him." Goethe's universe is so animate an organism that, as Hermann August Korff rightly claims, it is not really a universe but "a *universal process*, not an eternal being but a never-ending becoming, forming, and transforming."[22] Goethe himself put it thus: "God is active in what lives, not in what is dead; He is present in what is coming into existence and transforming itself, not in what is complete and solidified" (*GA* 24:316). The latter perishes because it violates the law of change, as we are told in the final lines of "Eins und Alles": "Denn alles muß in Nichts zerfallen, / Wenn es im Sein beharren will" (Everything that tries to persist in the form it has attained must perish; *GA* 1:514). But the force that created it remains inexhaustibly creative and thus is forever indestructible. "Nature," Goethe told Zelter, "is unceasingly active, profuse, and extravagant in order to insure that the Infinite be continuously present, since nothing can endure unchanged" (*GA* 21:996). The destruction of what appears static, however, is itself a transformation that ensures continued existence; the process of destruction is but another aspect of the process of creation. Accordingly, in the opening couplet of "Vermächtnis," which

21. Ibid., 167.
22. Wellek, *Concepts of Criticism*, 163; Hans Eichner, "The Rise of Modern Science and the Genesis of Romanticism," 15; Hermann August Korff, *Geist der Goethezeit*, 2:15.

immediately follows "Eins und Alles" in the "Gott und Welt" cycle, Goethe "corrected" the lines of poetry just quoted: "Kein Wesen kann zu nichts zerfallen! / Das Ewge regt sich fort in allen" (No being can perish! The eternal force animates all things; *GA* 1:514).

This validation of nature as a living, concrete reality corresponded to Goethe's deepest needs. He feared abstraction, as he stressed in his preface to the *Farbenlehre* ("die Abstraktion, vor der wir uns fürchten" [abstraction, which we stand in fear of]; *GA* 16:11). His mode of thinking was concrete (*gegenständlich*) in the sense that it always kept close to the objects (*Gegenstände*) of perception (*GA* 16:879). Even intuitions were to Goethe part of concrete experience, as is evident from his shock at Schiller's claim that the "archplant" (*Urpflanze*) was not a matter for observation, but an idea. If the *Urpflanze* was an idea, Goethe responded, it was an idea he could "see with his eyes" (*GA* 16:867–68). To put it differently, Goethe believed all his theorizing to be firmly rooted in his observation of the living reality of nature. This approach he referred to as his "dogged realism" (*hartnäckigen Realismus*; *GA* 16:868). He advocated a "sensitive empiricism" (*eine zarte Empirie*) that would enable the observer to identify himself utterly with the object and in this way to raise empiricism to the level of theory (*GA* 9:573).

Goethe's emphasis on nature's having reality and validity in its own right also distinguishes his position from that of the great philosophical pantheists of his day—Fichte, Schelling, and Hegel—all of whom reduced nature to playing a part of more or less importance in a dialectical process. Their primary focus lay elsewhere, as is evident from the terms dominating their philosophies—for instance, the Ego in Fichte and the *Geist* in Hegel. In Hegel's striking formula, nature is but an "Abfall der Idee von sich selbst," a "defection of the Idea from itself." Schelling's name, to be sure, is inseparably linked with German *Naturphilosophie*, but even Schelling saw *Natur* in the light of Kantian and Fichtean concepts.[23] The *Naturphilosophen*, Goethe told Schiller, start from above and work their way downward to nature (*GA* 20:593). Goethe did not want to think of nature or of nature's development in merely dialectical terms. During a conversation with Hegel about dialectic as a road to truth, he told his distinguished interlocutor that nature itself is "the infinite and eternal truth" (*GA* 24:669–70).

23. Georg Wilhelm Friedrich Hegel, *Enzyklopädie der philosophischen Wissenschaften im Grundrisse*, in *Sämtliche Werke*, 6:148; on Schelling, see Richard Kroner, *Von Kant bis Hegel*, 2:15–16.

It was this pantheistic naturalism, this sense of nature as a concretely present, all-encompassing divine force, that most impressed Emerson about Goethe, as it did Matthew Arnold.[24] The attraction for Emerson was twofold. First, Goethe's naturalism presented him with a view of nature far more complex and modern than the idealist or materialist views that had dominated Western thinking about nature from early Greek times.[25] Goethe kept nature firmly in the middle, so to speak: he denied that it was, on the one hand, an idealist abstraction or a mere antithesis in an idealist dialectic, or on the other, a materialist ultimate à la Holbach.[26] He insisted that nature was, at one and the same time, "Mind-pervaded" or "God-identical" and intensely "natural." Goethe's pantheism, to put it differently, was informed by tension between its "spiritual" side and its "natural" side. Or, to use one of his favorite concepts, his pantheism involved polarity. But polarity, it should be emphasized, is not dualism and thus does not in any way threaten Goethe's pantheistic monism. In Korff's words, "Polarity is duality-in-oneness, a unity of opposites either of which exists only by virtue of the other; polarity is, genetically speaking, a oneness that reaches apart because its essence is *tension*."[27]

Through the concept of polarity Goethe was thus able to maintain his pantheism—a monism by definition—while keeping it flexible and fluid. Both these characteristics of Goethean thought, the avoidance of dualism and the maintaining of dynamic tension, met deep-rooted Emersonian needs. As much as Goethe, Emerson feared man's alienation in a non-monistic universe. "If as Hedge thinks," he wrote in 1839, "I overlook great facts in stating the absolute laws of the soul; if as he seems to represent it the world is not . . . a bipolar Unity, but is *two*, is Me and It, then is there the Alien, the Unknown, and all we have believed & chanted out of our deep instinctive hope is a pretty dream" (*JMN* 7:200). Emerson, always striving to keep his thinking vital and dynamic, also found it easy to appreciate a bipolar pantheism that continually avoided coming to rest in either pole. Stephen E. Whicher has said that as a pantheist Emerson had only two choices: "one, pancosmism, the identification of God with the totality of things; the other, acosmism, the

24. R. H. Super, *The Time-Spirit of Matthew Arnold*, 65.

25. R. G. Collingwood, *The Idea of Nature*, 11–12.

26. For Goethe's horror at the deterministic "deadness" portrayed by Holbach's *Système de la nature*, see *GA* 10:537–38.

27. Korff, *Geist der Goethezeit*, 3:261.

denial of the reality of anything except God."[28] Goethe, however, confronted Emerson with a third choice: a pantheism that opted neither for pancosmism (pantheism with a materialistic emphasis) nor for acosmism (a pantheism—like Spinoza's, according to Hegel, or like Fichte's, according to Fichte himself—that accepts God or Spirit as the total reality), but which maintained a dynamic balance between the two.[29] Christopher Pearse Cranch understood Emerson's susceptibility to this Goethean position: "[Emerson] has no dealings with metaphysics. His mind seemed to shed Kant and Hegel as a duck sheds water. But he thought greatly of Goethe, for *he* harmonized the material and spiritual worlds. These two poles of the universe co-existed in perfect accord for Emerson." Henry Athanasius Brann, another nineteenth-century commentator, though less specific, is equally emphatic about the nature of Goethe's appeal for Emerson: "the pantheism of the German poet impregnates his whole mind."[30]

But given Emerson's idealistic background, it was inevitable that one of the poles of Goethe's pantheism, the "natural" one, should have been less familiar and therefore more intriguing to him; and this brings us to the second attraction that Goethe's pantheism held for Emerson. Goethe's sense of the concreteness, of the actual, all-pervasive presence of nature confronted Emerson with a view of reality that his philosophical background had predisposed him to depreciate. As one anonymous nineteenth-century critic put it, "If I were inclined to look for a flaw in Emerson's crystalline intellect, I should probably find it in a want of that due appreciation of the real, the eternal and necessary correlative of the ideal."[31] Better than anyone else, Goethe could help Emerson to a "due appreciation of the real." Goethe's "naturalism," Joseph Warren Beach has said, "was more steady and constant than . . . Wordsworth's." In fact, Goethe managed "more consistently than any other poet of his time, and with more circumstance and plausibility . . . to maintain the

28. Stephen E. Whicher, *Freedom and Fate: An Inner Life of Ralph Waldo Emerson*, 31.

29. Georg Wilhelm Friedrich Hegel, *Vorlesungen über die Geschichte der Philosophie*, in *Sämtliche Werke*, 19:372–74; Hegel's attribution of acosmism to Spinoza has come under attack: G. H. R. Parkinson, "Hegel, Pantheism, and Spinoza," *Journal of the History of Ideas* 38 (1977): 449–59; Johann Gottlieb Fichte, *Appellation an das Publicum*, in *Sämmtliche Werke*, 5:223–24.

30. Christopher Pearse Cranch, "Ralph Waldo Emerson," 214; Henry Athanasius Brann, "Hegel and his New England Echo," 227.

31. "Emerson's Essays," 598.

mind and spirit of man within the framework of nature."[32] Goethe was as little of a materialist as Emerson. He was as convinced as Emerson that Spirit pervades all. But being more authentically a poet than Emerson the essayist and more assiduously a student of natural phenomena than Emerson the transcendentalist, he was inclined more than Emerson to regard nature, in its concrete presence, as a complete incarnation of Spirit. Goethe's example, as Mary A. Wyman has pointed out, was a major factor in turning Emerson away "from extreme transcendentalism and subjectivity to a more objective view of . . . nature."[33] The revaluation of nature inherent in this view amounts to a critique of philosophical idealism, and the positions of Goethe and Emerson can be fully understood only in the context of their critique of idealism.

32. Joseph Warren Beach, *The Concept of Nature in Nineteenth-Century English Poetry*, 276.

33. Mary A. Wyman, *The Lure for Feeling in the Creative Process*, 43–44.

CHAPTER 3

THE CRITIQUE OF IDEALISM

As every student of Emerson knows, his general philosophical position is broadly identifiable as "idealism." He was, after all, the foremost representative of New England Transcendentalism, and according to his own definition, "Transcendentalism . . . is Idealism; Idealism as it appears in 1842" (*CW* 1:201). Moreover, given his tendency to regard the history of thought as a struggle between materialism and idealism, he of course considered himself a proponent of the latter. His language leaves no doubt about which side he preferred:

> Mankind have ever divided into two sects, Materialists and Idealists; the first class founding on experience, the second on consciousness; the first class beginning to think from the data of the senses, the second class perceive that the senses are not final, and say, the senses give us representations of things, but what are the things themselves, they cannot tell. The materialist insists on facts, on history, on the force of circumstances, and the animal wants of man; the idealist on the power of Thought and of Will, on inspiration, on miracle, on individual culture. (*CW* 1:201)

The materialist confidently assumes the objective validity of the content of his sensory perceptions; consequently, he has "a sort of instinctive belief in the absolute existence of nature." The idealist, on the other hand, attributes "necessary existence to spirit" and regards "nature as an accident and an effect" (*CW* 1:30). Idealism, to be sure, admits of degrees:

> We learn first to play with it academically, as the magnet was once a toy. Then we see in the heyday of youth and poetry that it may be true, that it is true in gleams and fragments. Then, its countenance waxes stern and grand, and we see that it must be true. It now shows itself ethical and practical. We learn that God IS; that he is in me; and that all things are shadows of him. The idealism of Berkeley is only a crude statement of the idealism of Jesus, and that, again, is a crude statement of the fact that all nature is the rapid efflux of goodness executing and organizing itself. (*CW* 2:183–84)

Passages like these suggest not only the very wide scope of Emerson's concept of idealism, but also his unsystematic approach. We find him

41

echoing tenets associated with Berkeley, Kant, Fichte, Plato, and Plotinus. Clearly, Emerson was interested in a flexible working philosophy rather than in systemic consistency. Emerson understood, moreover, that the most insidious form of slavery is enslavement to one's own ideology. He was, therefore, ultimately uncommitted to any philosophy. His concern was with thinking rather than with thought, with "the soul active" (*CW* 1:56) rather than with its products. It is quite in character that in *Nature*, his most ambitious attempt to express his theory of nature, he should espouse idealism while emphasizing that its validity is merely provisional. Since idealism accounts for nature "by other principles than those of carpentry and chemistry," he finds it, of course, infinitely preferable to materialism; nevertheless, he insists that idealism is "merely . . . a useful introductory hypothesis" (*CW* 1:37–38). His lecture on "The Transcendentalist" reveals, among other things, his considerable reservations about "Idealism as it appears in 1842." In the words of a recent critic, "What is puzzling about Emerson's writing . . . is his simultaneous attraction to and repulsion from idealism."[1] But perhaps this matter is not as puzzling as it seems. Influenced as Emerson's thinking was by his understandings concerning polarity and dialectic,[2] it was inevitable that the most incompatible ideas should have found a place in the hospitable universe of his mind and have functioned there in mutually fructifying tension. It is not surprising, therefore, that his thinking sometimes took directions quite incompatible with idealism. The importance of this "anti-idealism" in Emerson's thought has not been sufficiently appreciated.

Most relevant to my argument is the Platonic strain in Emerson's idealism. Like Plato, Emerson affirms the existence of a transcendent, absolute reality (called by Emerson "God" or "the Soul" or "Spirit" or "Reason" or "Mind" or "Thought") of which the phenomenal world (called by Emerson "Nature") is but an unstable and illusory reflection. In one of his many Platonic utterances, Emerson states that thought "fastens the attention upon immortal necessary uncreated natures, that is, upon Ideas; and in their beautiful and majestic presence, we feel that our outward being is a dream and a shade. Whilst we wait in this Olympus of gods, we think of nature as an appendix to the soul" (*CW* 1:34). Elsewhere we learn that "Mind is the only reality. . . . Nature, literature, history, are only subjective phenomena" (*CW* 1:203). Conse-

---

1. Anthony J. Cascardi, "Emerson on Nature: Philosophy beyond Kant," 202.
2. See Gustaaf Van Cromphout, "Emerson and the Dialectics of History."

quently, the search for reality involves a transcendence of nature: "The best, the happiest moments of life, are these delicious awakenings of the higher powers, and the reverential withdrawing of nature before its God" (CW 1:30). From the vantage point of thought, nature appears indeed a "degradation." The idealist affirms "facts which it only needs a retirement from the senses to discern," and such facts "assume a native superiority to material facts, degrading these into a language by which the first are to be spoken" (CW 1:201–2). Similarly, the idealist is "constrained to degrade persons into representatives of truths" (CW 1:203).

As *Nature* makes clear, however, Emerson could not remain satisfied with a theory which denies "substantive being to men and women" and which "makes nature foreign to me, and does not account for that consanguinity which we acknowledge to it" (CW 1:37–38). Idealism was valuable in apprising us of "the eternal distinction between the soul and the world" (CW 1:38). What was needed, however, was a way of establishing a relationship between the two that was more satisfying to man's sense of kinship with nature than was the Platonic relationship, according to which phenomena are but inadequate manifestations of ideal forms, of archetypes. What was needed, in other words, was a revaluation that would establish nature as the embodiment of the soul. Goethe's critique of idealism showed Emerson that it was possible to validate nature without denying spirit.

Goethe rejected "Idea" in the Platonic sense of a transcendent reality. The essential principle of Goethe's weltanschauung, Georg Simmel has said, is that "the idea is inherent in the phenomena."[3] Such immanence does not, however, make the Goethean idea any less awesome or significant than its Platonic counterpart. The idea, Goethe maintains, "is eternal and unique. . . . All that we become aware of and can express are only manifestations of the idea" (GA 9:539). But idea and manifestation—and here we depart radically from Platonism—are interdependent: "Der Schein, was ist er, dem das Wesen fehlt? / Das Wesen, wär es, wenn es nicht erschiene?" (What is manifestation without essence? But without manifestation, would essence even *be*?; GA 6:348). Goethe has no patience with transcendent speculation, which according to him produces but airy nothings (*Undinge*, GA 9:526). The idea has to be searched for *in* nature and *in* our experience. The idea is inseparable from its effects; only through its effects do we have a chance to grasp its essence. This is all the more true because Goethe, in his most drastic

3. Georg Simmel, *Goethe*, 121.

departure from Platonism, insists that the idea achieves its fullness *only through phenomenal realization.*

In the Platonic system, we remember, the world of phenomena inadequately reflects the realm of ideas, and the ideas—absolute, perfect, unchanging—remain unaffected by the inadequacy of their phenomenal representations. In Goethe's view, as Hermann Schmitz has shown at great length, it is the idea itself that is endangered by inadequate phenomenal realization.[4] The idea can be "saved" only if its realization constitutes a true "procreation" (*Zeugung*), a true "propagation" (*Fortpflanzung*). In such realization, Goethe maintains, "the begotten is not inferior to the begetter"; in fact, true procreation has this advantage, that "the begotten can excel the begetter" (*GA* 9:584). Or as he put it in an early letter, inverting the hierarchical order of Plotinian emanationism, "light is truth, even though the sun, from which light originates, is not truth" (*GA* 18:121). This theory accounts for much that is most characteristic of Goethe—for instance, his identification of truth with fruitfulness, already commented upon ("Was fruchtbar ist, allein ist wahr"; *GA* 1:515); his claim that the essence of human nature resides in man's inability to experience anything without becoming at once productive (*GA* 14:751); his assertion that the historical realization of an idea is the only test of its truth or falsehood (*GA* 21:73); and his indifference to anything unlikely to advance (*fördern*) his development (*GA* 16:880). This theory also provided a philosophical basis for his appreciation of nature: far from being a Hegelian "defection" (*Abfall*) from the idea, nature appears to be its necessary incarnation. It was Goethe's ultimate conviction that spirit depends for its existence on matter quite as much as matter depends for its existence on spirit.[5]

Emerson did not follow Goethe's philosophical reasoning in any detail. What he derived from Goethe was authoritative support for his understanding that nature possessed more essential reality than idealist philosophy (including Emerson's own variety of it) was willing to grant. One result was that Emerson, like Goethe, often used "Nature" in a sense hardly distinguishable from "Spirit." A few examples will

---

4. Hermann Schmitz, *Goethes Altersdenken im problemgeschichtlichen Zusammenhang*, especially 50–104. See also Ernst Cassirer, *Goethe und die geschichtliche Welt*, 120–24; Karl Viëtor, *Goethe the Poet*, 174; and Maurice Marache, *Le Symbole dans la pensée et l'oeuvre de Goethe*, 201–2.

5. Philipp Stein, ed., *Goethe-Briefe*, 8:251.

clarify. Discussing cosmogony and referring to theories of the prime mover, Emerson writes: "Nature . . . bestowed the impulse, and the balls rolled. . . . That famous aboriginal push propagates itself through all the balls of the system, and through every atom of every ball, through all the races of creatures, and through the history and performances of every individual" (CW 3:107). In "The Over-Soul" we are told that "new truth" and "great action" come out of "the heart of nature" (CW 2:166–67). The essay "Thoughts on Modern Literature" contains a passage of similar import: "The great lead us to Nature, and in our age to metaphysical Nature, to the invisible awful facts, to moral abstractions, which are not less Nature than is a river, or a coal-mine,—nay, they are far more Nature,—but its essence and soul" (W 12:315). Or note the strikingly paradoxical expression to be found in Emerson's first book: "Nature deif[ies] us" (CW 1:13). To the extent that man is evil, we learn from "Compensation," he "so far deceases from nature" (CW 2:70). But "Nature knows how to convert evil to good" (W 7:289–90). When, for instance, the Church of England had fallen into cant and hypocrisy, "Nature . . . had her remedy. Religious persons are driven out of the Established Church into sects, which instantly rise to credit and hold the Establishment in check" (W 5:228). Having discussed the decline of religion in his lecture on George Fox, Emerson continues: "But Nature never fails. Instantly the divine Light rekindles in some one or other obscure heart who denounces the deadness of the church and cries aloud for new and more appropriate practices" (EL 1:174). Emerson sometimes seems to regard nature as the force behind every positive development in history: "When nature has work to be done, she creates a genius to do it" (CW 1:128).

Statements like these are symptomatic of Emerson's "anti-idealist" recognition of nature as the locus of spirit. Though one could cite many passages from his works supporting an idealistic Spirit-Nature hierarchy, and though Emerson often considers transcendence of nature to be a prerequisite for an encounter with spirit, he at other times emphatically recognizes the equivalence of nature and spirit, and hence the possibility of man's encountering spirit in nature. "Once," to be sure, "men thought Spirit divine, and Matter diabolic," but "now science and philosophy recognize the parallelism, the approximation, the unity of the two" (W 10:213). The crescendo in the last sentence—parallelism, approximation, unity—reflects gradational, though not necessarily chronological, stages in Emerson's endeavor to discover spirit in nature. Only the third stage, however, fully validates nature. The first two stages, parallelism and approximation, are still compatible with an idealistic depreciation of nature, in the sense that nature can be regarded as only "mirroring" or, at most, "resembling" spirit. In the stage of unity, on the other hand, nature is spirit, or provides spirit with a chance to achieve phenomenal reality and in the process to "complete" itself. As Emerson puts it in one of his lectures, "it is needful that the soul should come out to the external world. It is imperfect until it does" (*EL* 2:311). There are different ways in which spirit achieves "natural" embodiment, in which "the world realizes the mind" (*W* 8:20), and in his examination of them Emerson closely follows Goethe.

Both writers recognize the *moment*, for example, as an incarnation of spirit.[6] In Goethe's conception, the moment not only eternalizes the temporal, but also temporalizes the eternal. His "eternal moment" (*Der Augenblick ist Ewigkeit*; *GA* 1:515) is neither an isolated segment of time nor a rising above time into an atemporal eternity. Instead, the moment is eternity embedded in the fullness of time. "Every moment," Goethe told Eckermann, "has infinite worth because it is the representative [*Repräsentant*] of all eternity" (*GA* 24:67). The moment thus constitutes the fusion of time and eternity, or more precisely, the moment is eternity realizing itself in time.[7] Though the inspired moment was a central preoccupation in Romantic (and much post-Romantic) literature,[8] Emerson's approach to it is Goethean in that he often emphasizes eternity's immanence in the moment rather than the moment as a means of transcendence. Commenting upon a French sentence that he copied from a passage in *Dichtung und Wahrheit*, in which Goethe praises moments of insight (*GA* 10:745; *JMN* 11:298 n. 64), Emerson concludes: "Moments of insight . . . what ample borrowers of eternity they are!" (*W* 7:178). Like Goethe, Emerson thus sees the moment absorbing eternity. The moment, as a result, contains *essential* reality: "This shining moment is an edifice / Which the Omnipotent cannot rebuild" (*W* 9:350). The moment, indeed, contains so much essential reality that it partakes of the ineffability of the universal: "The good moments . . . do

6. Goethe, we have seen, uses the term "idea" (*Idee*) rather than "spirit" (*Geist*) in the context under discussion here; but since he emphasizes the eternity and uniqueness of the idea and advises against using the term "idea" in the plural (*GA* 9:539), it seems reasonable to use "spirit" and "idea" interchangeably.

7. See Gundolf, *Goethe*, 266; Peter Eichhorn, *Idee und Erfahrung im Spätwerk Goethes*, 157–59; and Schmitz, *Goethes Altersdenken*, 148–67.

8. See M. H. Abrams, *Natural Supernaturalism: Tradition and Revolution in Romantic Literature*, 385–90, 418–27.

not belong to genius but to Man. They refuse to be recorded" (*JMN* 6:248). Hence "Today," which Emerson often equates with the living moment, is "rolled up & muffled in impenetrable folds" (*JMN* 13:298). But given the moment's, or today's, encapsulation of spirit, what we need above all is "insight into to-day" (*CW* 1:67). "The most learned scholar," therefore, is not he "who can unearth for me the buried dynasties of Sesostris and Ptolemy, the Sothiac era, the Olympiads and consulships, but who can unfold the theory of this particular Wednesday" (*W* 7:179). What all this amounts to is that often Emerson is more interested in the moment's power to validate Nature (in Emerson's inclusive, philosophical sense of the term, i.e., all that is not Spirit) than in the moment as a transcendent revelation of Spirit. The moment transfigures the most insignificant fact:

> Day creeps after day, each full of facts, dull, strange, despised things that we cannot enough despise, call heavy, prosaic, and desart. . . . Presently the aroused intellect finds gold and gems in one of these scorned facts, then finds that the day of facts is a rock of diamonds, that a fact is an Epiphany of God, that on every fact of his life he should rear a temple of wonder and joy; that in going to eat meat, to buy or to sell; to meet a friend or thwart an adversary, to communicate a piece of news or to give a gift he celebrates the arrival of an inconceivably remote purpose and law at last on the shores of Being and into the ripeness and domain of Nature. (*EL* 3:47–48)

In Goethean fashion, Emerson here concludes with the assertion that common facts and experiences, transmuted by moments of insight, are the means by which the "inconceivably remote" laws and purposes of Spirit arrive at reality ("the shores of Being") and achieve completeness ("the ripeness . . . of Nature").

Another mode in which Spirit realizes itself and ipso facto validates Nature is action. Symptomatic of the central importance of action in Goethe's thought is the famous passage in which Faust struggles with the meaning of the opening line of the Gospel according to St. John (*Faust*, lines 1224–37; *GA* 5:180–81). Endeavoring to produce an adequate translation, Faust rejects his first version—"In the beginning was the Word!"—as utterly unsatisfactory. His next attempt—"In the beginning was the Sense" (*der Sinn*)—fails to satisfy him because he cannot convince himself that Sense (i.e., meaning, thought) is the source of all action and creativity ("Ist es der Sinn, der alles wirkt und schafft?"). An obvious improvement is the change of "Sense" to "Force" (*Kraft*)—"In the beginning was the Force!"—but even this translation does not please Faust. At last the truth flashes upon him: "In the beginning was the

Deed!" ("Im Anfang war die Tat!"). The significance of this understanding of *Logos* as Deed becomes fully apparent when we recall that in his opening sentence St. John identified *Logos* with God. Equally expressive of the centrality of action in Goethe's thought are the words of the Chorus Mysticus at the end of *Faust, Part Two*, where deficiency (*das Unzulängliche*) and ineffability (*das Unbeschreibliche*) find their divine realization in event and deed:

> Das Unzulängliche,
> Hier wird's Ereignis;
> Das Unbeschreibliche,
> Hier ist's getan.
> (*GA* 5:526, lines 12106–9)

For Goethe, Wilhelm Emrich has remarked, "the ineffable falls neither within a reflective-theoretical nor within a dogmatic-meditative purview; it pertains exclusively to the sphere of action. . . . The deed . . . is the only guarantee both of the salvation and 'event-becoming' of deficiency, and of the manifestation of ineffability."[9]

This emphasis on action is thus clearly an aspect of Goethe's belief that the Idea depends for its "survival" on productive phenomenal realization. The Idea must accomplish "its divine mission—to be productive" (*GA* 9:519), and it is man's duty to realize the Idea as fully as possible through his own productivity. Goethe claimed repeatedly that his own thinking acquired shape and meaning only through action: "Da ich nur handelnd denken kann" (Inasmuch as I can think only while active; *GA* 20:580); "Da ich nur denken kann insofern ich produziere" (Since I can think only insofar as I am productive; *GA* 19:365–66). What matters here is not so much anything accomplished through action, but action itself—unceasing activity in an ever-present Now: "Das Tun interessiert, / Das Getane nicht" (Doing interests us, not what is done; *GA* 1:612). The Idea, being infinite, realizes itself through action that is endless. Action thus becomes a *Streben nach dem Unendlichen*, a ceaseless striving to attain the unattainable. In other words, man's immortal idealistic longings (*Sehnsucht*) "must be ever productive" (*GA* 23:315); *Sehnsucht* finds its "fulfillment" in action ever transcending itself. The highest vocation of man, therefore, is to be active: "Tätig zu sein . . . ist des Menschen erste Bestimmung," we are told in *Wilhelm Meisters Lehrjahre*, the archetypal bildungsroman (*GA* 7:447). Furthermore, it is

9. Wilhelm Emrich, *Die Symbolik von "Faust II,"* 420.

through action that man acquires some understanding of the Idea within him: "How can one get to know oneself? Never through contemplation, but through action" (GA 9:554). It is through unceasing action that this human Idea ultimately prevails and is "saved" (Faust, GA 5:520, lines 11936–37).

   Like Goethe, Emerson often regards action as necessary to the realization of Spirit. Even for the Scholar—that is, Man Thinking, the delegated intellect (CW 1:53)—action is "essential" because without action "thought can never ripen into truth" (CW 1:59). Indeed, without action thought cannot even ripen into thought: "The preamble of thought, the transition through which it passes from the unconscious to the conscious, is action" (CW 1:59). Or as Emerson puts it in his essay on "Intellect," "When the spiritual energy is directed on something outward, then it is a thought" (CW 2:199). Action gives definition to the unconscious: "In love, in art, in avarice, in politics, in labor, in games, we study to utter our painful secret. The man is only half himself, the other half is his expression" (CW 3:4). In his very first book Emerson had already affirmed that "an action is the perfection and publication of thought" (CW 1:28; my italics). The discipline of nature is intended, Emerson says in a strikingly Goethean phrase, "to form the Hand of the mind" (CW 1:24). Though the ancients had compared the hand to the mind, as Goethe knew (GA 9:649),[10] he went beyond earlier comparisons by making the hand (or the arm) a metaphor for the mind's self-realization, as when Wilhelm Meister talks of his failure to realize his greatest hopes as a crushing of "the arms of [his] mind [die Arme meines Geistes] . . . with which [he] reached toward infinity" (GA 7:90). Similarly, for Emerson the spirit realizes itself through "the Hand," through action in and upon nature. Needless to say, for Emerson as for Goethe such realization remains forever incomplete. "The natural philosophy

   10. The connection between the two seems to have been assumed almost universally, as is indicated by the fact that such verbs as Greek lambanō, Latin comprehendo, German (be)greifen, and English grasp refer to both physical and intellectual acquiring. A seventeenth-century Puritan, describing men's apprehension (another "dual" term) of an idea, writes: "They gather it up with the hands of their understandings" (quoted in Perry Miller, The New England Mind: The Seventeenth Century [1939; reprint, Cambridge: Harvard University Press, 1967], 148). Sir Thomas Browne writes in Pseudodoxia Epidemica that the "immediate determination and efficiency" of crystal are "wrought by the hand of its concretive spirit" (The Works of Sir Thomas Browne, ed. Geoffrey Keynes, 4 vols. [1928–31; reprint, London: Faber & Faber, 1964], 2:86).

that now is," to take an important modern achievement, "is only the first gropings of [the soul's] gigantic hand" (*CW* 1:55). But however incomplete the achievement to which action is directed, the truth remains that as a mode of realization action is "total," whereas thinking is only "partial" (*CW* 1:61).

Action acquires additional validation through its being the opposite of thought in Goethean and Emersonian concepts of polarity. In polarity, we remember, each pole can exist only by virtue of the existence of the other, and each pole achieves meaning only through its opposition to the other. Both poles are thus equivalent in their reciprocal necessity and, constituting a unity-through-opposition, are mutually completive. Emerson explains this concept in *The American Scholar*: "That great principle of Undulation in nature, that shows itself in the inspiring and expiring of the breath; in desire and satiety; in the ebb and flow of the sea, in day and night, in heat and cold, and as yet more deeply ingrained in every atom and every fluid, is known to us under the name of Polarity." Polarity is "the law of nature because [it is] the law of spirit" (*CW* 1:61). Goethe, whose commitment to the doctrine of polarity was perhaps deeper than that of any other Romantic,[11] often made action the polar counterpart of thought. In *Wilhelm Meisters Lehrjahre*, for instance, mind and action cultivated separately lead to human incompleteness: "Der Sinn erweitert, aber lähmt; die Tat belebt, aber beschränkt" (The mind expands, but inactivates; action quickens, but restricts; *GA* 7:590). *Bildung* involves a mutually fructifying tension between the two. As we learn from *Wilhelm Meisters Wanderjahre*, "Thinking and doing, doing and thinking, that is the sum of all wisdom." In fact, whoever "puts action to the test of thought, and thought to the test of action, cannot err" (*GA* 8:285). As Barker Fairley has said, Goethe insists that "it is as futile to act . . . without thinking as it is to think without acting."[12]

Emerson in similar fashion validates action through polarity. He follows the passage just quoted from *The American Scholar* with the statement that "the mind now thinks; now acts; and each fit reproduces the other" (*CW* 1:61). A journal entry of 1848 reads: "Action & idea are man & woman, both indispensable" (*JMN* 11:53). Emerson's view that words and deeds "are quite indifferent modes of the divine energy"—

11. See McFarland, *Romanticism and the Forms of Ruin*, 302–7; and Wahr, *Emerson and Goethe*, 123–24.

12. Fairley, *Study of Goethe*, 266.

words being "also actions, and actions . . . a kind of words" (*CW* 3:6)—helps clarify a passage in *Nature* where he dramatizes the Spirit's achieving self-knowledge through polarity with its self-expressive actions:

> Words and actions are not the attributes of mute and brute nature. They introduce us to the human form, of which all other organizations appear to be degradations. When this organization appears among so many that surround it, the spirit prefers it to all others. It says, "From such as this, have I drawn joy and knowledge. In such as this, have I found and beheld myself. I will speak to it. It can speak again. It can yield me thought already formed and alive." (*CW* 1:28)

Fact, incidentally, parallels action in that it also is validated through its polar relation to thought: "Every day's doubt is whether to seek for Ideas or to collect facts. For all successful study is the marriage of thoughts & things. A continual reaction of the thought classifying the facts & of facts suggesting the thought" (*JMN* 5:72).

Emerson further agrees with Goethe that action itself is more important than anything accomplished through it. As every reader of Emerson knows, his interest does not lie in anything "complete" but in the never-ceasing *process* of realization: "The one thing in the world of value, is, the active soul." It is "the soul active" that "utters truth, or creates," and "in this action, it is genius" (*CW* 1:56). The mode of power is transition since "power ceases in the instant of repose" (*W* 12:59; *CW* 2:40). Not surprisingly, Emerson's God, a God that "speaketh, not spake" (*CW* 1:89), offers everyone a choice "between truth and repose" (*CW* 2:202).

In addition to the moment and action there is a third factor which Goethe and Emerson perceive as validating nature. What I have in mind is suggested by a passage in *Nature* that Emerson quotes from Goethe: "The wise man, in doing one thing, does all; or, in the one thing he does rightly, he sees the likeness of all which is done rightly" (*CW* 1:28; *JMN* 5:128 n. 392; *GA* 8:43). Action, as we saw, defines and hence restricts (*beschränkt*). On the other hand, as the passage just quoted indicates, a right action has universal implications. Seen this way, action points to one of Goethe's (and Emerson's) basic convictions: the identity of the one and the many, of the specific and the general, of the individual and totality. Goethe, rejecting abstract categories and large generic concepts as meaningless, considered the concrete instance itself to contain universality. According to one of his *Maximen*, "The particular and the universal coincide: the particular is the universal appearing under distinct conditions" (*GA* 9:573). Or in paradoxical condensation: "What is the universal? The single instance" ("Was ist das Allgemeine? Der einzelne Fall"; *GA* 9:572). In this matter, Goethe's thinking, as Hermann Schmitz has pointed out, is hardly distinguishable from Hegel's concrete universal (*das konkrete Allgemeine*), in which the universal is not an abstract concept separate from the particular (*abstract*, after all, is derived from Latin *abstrahere*: to draw away, to detach) but instead constitutes with the particular a union informed by dialectical tension.[13] In Goethe's view, particular and universal form an intensely vital union animated by dynamic polarity:

> Fundamental character of the living unit: to divide itself, to reunify itself, to become part of universality, to persist in its particularity, to transmute itself, to individualize itself, and, as may be the case with life under a thousand different conditions, to appear and to disappear, to harden and to melt, to solidify and to flow, to expand and to contract. Since all these activities take place concurrently, one and all are present at any given moment. Emerging and perishing, creation and destruction, birth and death, pleasure and pain—all interact in the same sense and in the same degree. Consequently, even the most particular occurrence always appears as an image and symbol of the universal. (*GA* 9:573-74)

Most relevant to our investigation is the high value which the particular thus acquires. By stressing the concreteness of the appearance of the universal principle, by emphasizing that the concrete instance contains universality, Goethe once again validates nature.

This particular mode of validation is inseparable from Goethe's (and Emerson's) pantheism. In Thomas McFarland's words, "the final equation of pantheism," "the alpha and omega of pantheism," is "the identity of the One and the Many." In the pantheistic view of reality, "All is One and One is All."[14] Emerson expresses this view emphatically: "The true doctrine of omnipresence is, that God re-appears with all his parts in every moss and cobweb. The value of the universe contrives to throw itself into every point" (*CW* 2:60). Put tersely, "All is in Each" (*JMN* 5:136). It is possible, as Edward Waldo Emerson maintains (*W* 1:409-10), that Emerson was indebted for this doctrine to the *hen kai pan* (One and All) of Xenophanes. But his statements so often refer to Goethe or have a Goethean ring to them or are direct quotations from Goethe, such as the statement already cited from *Nature* on one right

---

13. Schmitz, *Goethes Altersdenken*, 41.
14. McFarland, *Coleridge and the Pantheist Tradition*, 68, 69, 282.

action representing all right action, that one must conclude that he regarded Goethe as the man who made the doctrine relevant to modern concerns. A few examples selected from an 1835–1836 journal will help substantiate this view:

> The universal fact, says Goethe, is that which takes place once. Well, let us read in the same faith, that the sentence now under the eyes is one of universal application, and the volume in our hand is for us the voice of God & Time. (*JMN* 5:149)

> Goethe moralizes on the Roman Carnival, and shows it as an emblem of human life. And so is every feast, & every assembly, and every institution—, and every work and every spectacle. . . . A nation represents the world; a town the world; a family, the world; a man, the world. . . . A Day is a miniature Eternity; an hour, a moment, is the same. A child's game hints to an intelligent beholder all the attributes of the Supreme Being. (*JMN* 5:142)

> Only last evening I found the following sentence in Goethe, a comment and consent to my speculations on the All in Each in Nature this last week.
> "Every existing thing is an analogon of all existing things. Thence appears to us Being ever, at once sundered & connected. If we follow the analogy too far all things confound themselves in identity. If we avoid it, then all things scatter into infinity. In both cases, observation is at a stand, in one as too lively, in the other as dead." Vol. 22, p. 245 [*GA* 8:323].
> Man is an analogist. And therefore no man loses any time or any means who studies that one thing that is before him, though a log or a snail. (*JMN* 5:138)

> Every primal Truth is alone an expression of all Nature. . . . A leaf is a compend of Nature, and Nature a colossal leaf. . . . Hence Goethe's striving to find the Arch-plant. (*JMN* 5:137–38)

The ideas here expressed, or variations upon them, recur often in Emerson's works. Invariably their aim or effect is to concretize a universal law or principle and thus to enhance the value of the concrete, as when Emerson says that "all the laws of nature may be read in the smallest fact" (*CW* 2:201); that "the universe is represented in every one of its particles" (*CW* 2:59); that "whatever one act we do, whatever one thing we learn, we are doing and learning all things,—marching in the direction of universal power" (*W* 8:23); or that "every man is an inlet to the [universal mind] and to all of the same" (*CW* 2:3). One of the fullest statements of this principle occurs in *Nature*: "Every particular in nature, a leaf, a drop, a crystal, a moment of time is related to the whole, and partakes of the perfection of the whole. Each particle is a microcosm, and faithfully renders the likeness of the world" (*CW* 1:27). As is so often the case, however, Emerson here but echoes and extends an observation of Goethe's, which he had copied in his journal in 1834: "The smallest production of nature has the circle of its completeness within itself. . . . I am perfectly sure that within this circle however narrow, an entirely genuine existence is enclosed" (*JMN* 6:114; *GA* 19:45).[15] Views like these also played an important part in Goethe's and Emerson's aesthetics.

15. See Stanley M. Vogel, *German Literary Influences on the American Transcendentalists*, 103.

CHAPTER 4

THE VISUAL ARTS

An account of Goethe's aesthetics that would do justice to the complexity of the subject would require a careful investigation of the changes in his views during the sixty years that he expressed himself on matters artistic. The aesthetic views of the young Goethe and those that he voiced during and for many years after his first Italian journey (September 1786–May 1788) are considerably different. And just as there is an *Altersstil*, a "late style," distinguishing the literary productions of Goethe's later years, so there is also an *Altersstil* in his aesthetic thinking during his last two decades or so. Such an account would not much advance, however, an examination of the significance for Emerson of Goethe's aesthetic theories. As a creative thinker Emerson borrowed, in this field as in others, such elements from Goethe as harmonized with and were likely to advance his own thought. Such borrowing is, by definition, eclectic. Looking primarily for "inspiration," Emerson was indifferent as to whether the inspiring element was early or late Goethe, or even whether it was central or peripheral to Goethe's thinking. In a sense, Goethe invited such indifference. He provided no aesthetic system (unlike, say, Kant, Hegel, or Solger); instead, he left a wealth of fascinating ideas and theories enriched and supported by years of examination, interpretation, and emulation of works of art. For, unlike Emerson, Goethe was as profoundly interested in works of art as in Art, and he was a practitioner of the visual arts as well as a theoretician, as is shown by, among other things, his roughly two thousand surviving drawings and sketches.

Such obvious differences between them notwithstanding, Emerson regarded Goethe as the foremost authority on the subject of art. Though Goethe offers his readers "fine things" on almost any subject, Emerson writes, he "seems to speak of nothing so wisely as of Art" (*L* 2:100). Indeed, his essays on art "vindicat[e] his claim to the largest share of good sense possessed by his contemporaries" (*L* 3:285–86). Conspicuous among Goethe's cultural achievements, we learn in *Representative Men*, is "his penetration of every secret of the Fine Arts" (*CW* 4:164). Furthermore, Goethe "has explained the distinction between the antique and the modern spirit and art." As Emerson puts it with laconic finality,

Goethe "has defined Art, its scope and laws" (*CW* 4:158). Obviously Goethe was someone from whom an aesthetically half-starved New Englander like Emerson could learn much.

Goethe was Emerson's mentor during the latter's first sustained experience of art. When Emerson visited Italy in 1833, Goethe's *Italienische Reise* served him as a guide to the country's artistic treasures. Goethe helped Emerson develop a less moralistic, more liberal and sympathetic attitude toward art. There is little evidence, however, that Goethe deepened Emerson's appreciation of actual works of art to any significant degree. Whereas Goethe's aesthetic theorizing was continually reinforced by his probing evaluations of specific works, Emerson's theoretical endeavors seem hardly ever to have benefited from his encounters with architectural, sculptural, or pictorial masterpieces. Approve as he did of Goethe's "excellent rule . . . that you should not speak of works of art except in their presence" (*JMN* 7:17; *GA* 11:410), Emerson perhaps recognized that, given the relative brevity of his encounters with masterpieces, he was in no position to provide significant insights into them. Or perhaps Henry James was right, after all, when he commented on Emerson's insensitivity to works of art as they visited the Louvre and the Vatican: "there were certain chords in Emerson that did not vibrate at all."[1] At any rate, Emerson's remarks on specific works of art are disappointingly superficial, and his experience of such works seems to have borne little fruit in his aesthetic thought.

Goethe's contribution to Emerson's thinking was, therefore, almost exclusively theoretical. The *Italienische Reise*, Goethe's numerous essays in art history and art criticism, and the even more numerous aesthetic aperçus to be found in his novels, poems, plays, letters, conversations, biographical sketches, and autobiographical writings confronted Emerson with a body of aesthetic thought unmatched, at the time, in range and versatility. Its effect upon Emerson eclipsed any other influence upon him in the field of aesthetics. "Without minimizing the effect of other writers upon Emerson," Vivian C. Hopkins has said, "one must grant that Goethe represented the greatest single influence upon his aesthetic theory. . . . Goethe laid the foundation for Emerson's theory of art and literature." René Wellek is equally emphatic in calling Goethe "the source of [Emerson's] aesthetics" and in pointing out that Emerson returned to Goethe "over and over again . . . for his theory of art."[2]

1. Henry James, "Emerson," 74.
2. Hopkins, "Influence of Goethe," 342; René Wellek, *A History of Modern Criti-*

No theoretical task seemed more important to both Goethe and Emerson than to clarify the connection between Art and Nature. Karl Viëtor's words about Goethe could be spoken with equal justice about Emerson: "On no aesthetic problem did Goethe ponder so much, about none did he speak so much, as on that of the mutual relation of Nature and art."[3] As we saw in chapter 2, there is an aesthetic aspect to Goethe's and Emerson's modes of viewing nature. Goethe went so far as to say that "a work of nature should be treated as a work of art" (GA 12:344). Conversely, as will become clear in this chapter, both writers found it impossible to treat the principles of art in isolation from the laws of nature. Hopkins might have said about Goethe what she says about Emerson: "underlying his theory of art is his concept of nature."[4] Inverting the statement quoted above, Goethe also maintained that "a work of art should be treated as a work of nature" (GA 12:344).

Needless to say, neither Goethe nor Emerson thought of the relation of art to nature as one of "imitation" in the neoclassical sense. M. H. Abrams has reminded us that in the eighteenth century "the tenet that art is an imitation seemed almost too obvious to need iteration or proof."[5] Goethe, however, complained about "the half-true gospel of the imitation of nature, so pleasing to all who merely trust their senses and are not conscious of what lies behind" (GA 15:1027). Great art, according to Goethe, was an *idealized re-production* of nature. In Goethe's theory the principle that art idealizes nature had a meaning very different, however, from the meanings attached to it in neoclassical interpretations, as, for instance, in *la belle nature* of Charles Perrault and Charles Batteux, or in Dryden's and Pope's identification of nature with sound reason and the rules, or in the "general nature" of Roger de Piles and Samuel Johnson. The artist, in Goethe's view, has to seize, through intuition, the idea that nature is trying to develop in various forms (among them the human figure), and reproduce that idea in his art. There are, consequently, two aspects to this principle. In the first place, the artist's mind—the human mind—is, as we saw in chapter 2, analogous to the mind active in nature and is, therefore, capable of grasping nature's "idea." Hence Goethe's paradoxical statement: "A consummate work of art is a work of the

---

cism, 1750–1950, 3:175.

3. Karl Viëtor, *Goethe the Thinker*, 166.

4. Vivian C. Hopkins, *Spires of Form: A Study of Emerson's Aesthetic Theory*, 6.

5. M. H. Abrams, *The Mirror and the Lamp: Romantic Theory and the Critical Tradition*, 11.

human spirit, and in this sense also a work of nature" (*GA* 13:180). Second, the artist, guided by the forms of nature, strives to give form to nature's idea in his art. He does not, however, copy the forms of nature. "Re-production" requires insight into the methods through which nature produces its forms in the first place. This brings us to Goethe's genetic conception of art: the artist has not only to intuit nature's idea but also to grasp the idea's *formal development*. As artists we can emulate nature, Goethe says, "only when we have at least to some extent learned from her the manner in which she proceeds in the formation of her works" (*GA* 13:180). Emerson recognized the wisdom of this approach. Commenting upon the inadequacy of "works of human art" in comparison with "natural structures," he concluded: "Therefore Goethe, whose whole life was a study of the theory of art, said no man should be admitted to his Republic, who was not versed in Natural History" (*W* 12:160–61; cf. *EL* 1:72).

Goethe's theory of art is thus clearly rooted in his revolutionary approach to nature. As Ernst Cassirer has pointed out, Goethe "completed the transition from the previous *generic* view to the modern *genetic* view of organic nature." Whereas the generic view classified the products of a natural world in which "nothing could come to be except what already was" (*GA* 12:373), the genetic view perceived nature as an endlessly creative process. Goethe created "a new ideal of knowledge," Cassirer says, not only by being the first to coin the word "morphology," but also by making his morphological theories culminate in "metamorphosis."[6] Morphology became for Goethe essentially the theory of "the formation and transformation of organisms" (*GA* 17:115).

Goethe's years of study in organic science, especially botany and anatomy, bore rich aesthetic fruit as early as the opening stages of his first Italian journey. As Barker Fairley points out, "the organic point of view that we find in [his] early comments on Verona, Venice, and Rome holds good for the Italian journey as a whole, and not only for the Italian journey but for the rest of his life."[7] Goethe's scientific experience gave concreteness and depth to his aesthetic speculations. He was, after all, as Abrams says, "distinctive among aesthetic organologists in that he was himself a research biologist as well as a theorist of art. He deliberately pursued these as mutually illuminating kinds of activity, each new hypothesis or discovery he made in biology duly reappearing in the form of

6. Ernst Cassirer, *Rousseau, Kant and Goethe*, 68, 69, 73.
7. Fairley, *Study of Goethe*, 127–28.

new organizing principles or insights in the field of his criticism."[8] Emerson observed Goethe's organic theory, with its genetic, developmental, metamorphic emphases, at work in the *Italienische Reise*:

> It is a favorite work of Goethe to give a theory of every institution, art, artwork, custom which he observes. Thus his explanation of the Italian Time-measure as *growing out of* Italian climate; of the Obelisk of Egypt as *growing out of* a common natural fracture in the granite parallelopiped [*sic*] in upper Egypt; of the Doric Architecture and the Gothic; of the Venetian music of the Gondolier *originating in* the habit of the fishers' wives of the Lido singing to their husbands on the sea; of the Amphitheatre which is the *natural cup that forms round* every sight in the street; of the coloring of Titian & Paul Veronese, which one may see in daylight in Venice day by day. (*JMN* 5:132; my italics)

Goethe's commitment to organicism is further illustrated by his distaste for the French loanword *Komposition*. The term, whose literal meaning is "putting together," should be applied, Goethe says, to things like machines, which are put together piece by piece. Unfortunately the French apply it to both nature and art. The term is meaningless when it refers to the productions of nature (*Erzeugnisse der Natur*) because these are not put together mechanically but instead are "organic wholes," all parts of which are engaged in "vital self-formation" and pervaded by "a unifying spirit." Similarly, the term is also objectionable in reference to art. "How can one say," Goethe exclaims to Eckermann, "that Mozart composed *Don Juan*! Composition! As if it were a cake or biscuits whipped together out of eggs, flour, and sugar!" Far from being "pieced together," *Don Juan* "as a whole and in every part is pervaded by one spirit and one soul, and by the breath of one life" (*GA* 24:759).

For Goethe, in sum, a work of art is nature growing toward "perfection" through the genius of nature's highest product: man. As Abrams aptly puts it, Goethe saw "artistic invention as a process of nature within the realm of mind."[9] The artist re-expresses nature's deepest striving, the striving to attain to form (*Gestalt*). Goethe, the universal morphologist, regarded all the operations of nature as stages in a dynamic pursuit of form.[10] Similarly, "man is formative by nature. . . . As soon as his existence is assured . . . he grasps about him for material to breathe his

---

8. Abrams, *Mirror and the Lamp*, 206.
9. Ibid.
10. See Adolf Meyer-Abich, *Die Vollendung der Morphologie Goethes durch Alexander von Humboldt*.

spirit into" (*GA* 13:24). Goethe was particularly emphatic on these points. He claimed that "the highest, the only activity of nature and of art is the creation of forms," or *Gestaltung* (*GA* 19:566).

As already suggested, Goethe believed that art sometimes surpasses nature. Man, the most advanced result of nature's perpetual striving for self-enhancement (*Steigerung*), continues this process of self-enhancement by rising to the production of art (*GA* 13:421–22). Great art is, at one and the same time, "natural" and "more than natural." It is based "on our deepest perceptions, on the essence of things, insofar as we are able to grasp this essence through visible and tangible forms," i.e, through nature (*GA* 13:68). But in order really to grasp the essence of nature, which is also the essence of *his* nature, the artist must penetrate not only "the depth of things" but also "the depth of his own soul." Only thus will he be able "to produce, in rivalry with nature, something spiritually organic (*etwas geistig Organisches*), and to give his work such a content and form as to make it appear at once natural and supra-natural" (*GA* 13:141–42). As Goethe says elsewhere, the artist, having been produced by nature, in his turn produces "a second nature, but a felt, thought out, and humanly perfected one" (*GA* 13:210). Art, therefore, is idealistic in content and idealized in form. "The highest task of every art," we are told in *Dichtung und Wahrheit*, "is to create through representation the appearance of a higher reality" (*GA* 10:534). Yet this higher reality does not divorce art from nature. The work of art is "above nature, but not out of nature" (*übernatürlich, aber nicht außernatürlich*; *GA* 13:180). Art is nature's deepest insight into itself. Therefore, "anyone to whom nature has begun to reveal her open secret [*offenbares Geheimnis*] experiences an irresistible longing for nature's worthiest interpreter—art" (*GA* 9:518).

Emerson echoes these Goethean views repeatedly in journals, lectures, and essays. Many of his most emphatic and most characteristically "Emersonian" statements on art are reexpressions of Goethean ideas. For Emerson also, art is a product of "Ideal Nature" (*W* 7:48), and as such it incarnates the universal law of *Steigerung*: "Art seeks not nature but the ideal which nature herself strives after" (*JMN* 5:417). In February 1836 Emerson translated, somewhat awkwardly, one of the most important statements on aesthetics in the *Italienische Reise*: "These great Art-works are, like the highest works upon Nature of Man, after true & natural laws executed. Everything arbitrary, fanciful perishes: Where is Necessity there is God" (*JMN* 5:129; *GA* 11:436). "Necessity," inherent in "true & natural laws," becomes a key concept in Emerson's aesthetics.

He speaks of "the necessity that reigns in all the kingdom of Art. Arising out of eternal Reason, one and perfect, whatever is beautiful rests on the foundation of the necessary. Nothing is arbitrary, nothing is insulated in beauty" (W 7:52). Or let us consider this passage:

> We feel, in seeing a noble building, which rhymes well, as we do in hearing a perfect song, that it is spiritually organic [cf. Goethe's *etwas geistig Organisches* above]; that is, had a necessity, in Nature, for being . . . and is now only discovered and executed by the artist, not arbitrarily composed by him [cf. Goethe on *Komposition*]. And so every genuine work of art has as much reason for being as the earth and the sun. (W 7:53)

In other words, a work of art "must be strictly subordinated to the laws of Nature, so as to become a sort of continuation and in no wise a contradiction of Nature" (W 7:48; cf. Goethe's *übernatürlich, aber nicht außernatürlich* above).

Emerson also follows Goethe in regarding art as rooted in the dynamic, metamorphic laws of nature. A work of art reveals "the mind that formed Nature, again in active operation" (W 7:51). In the mind of the artist, "the beauty of nature reforms itself . . . not for barren contemplation, but for new creation," for embodiment "in new forms" (CW 1:16). Art, in other words, is "nature passed through the alembic of man" (CW 1:17). Hence, "the production of a work of art" not only is "the result or expression of nature," but also "throws light upon the mystery of humanity" (CW 1:16–17). Human creativity, Emerson notes in an essay on art, is "nature's finer success in self-explication" (CW 2:209). The beauty of art, therefore, transcends the beauty of nature: "the beauty of things . . . becomes a new, and higher beauty, when expressed" (CW 3:8). This is what Goethe had in mind when he said that the integrity of a work of art arises from the artist's spirit rather than from nature (GA 24:623). Contemplation of the "higher beauty" of art does not, however, separate us from nature, but leads us back to it. In his journal Emerson translated a passage from the *Italienische Reise* which throws light upon the mode of this return to nature: "And so is our eye thro' works of art gradually so tuned that we become ever more eager for the presence of Nature & more susceptible of the beauties which she offers us" (JMN 6:214; GA 11:444–45). Stated more succinctly this idea becomes part of Emerson's argument in another essay on art: "a study of admirable works of art sharpens our perceptions of the beauty of Nature" (W 7:51). Aesthetic perception thus "sharpened" enables us to appreciate nature itself as the greatest work of art: "In happy hours, nature appears to us one with art; art perfected,—the work of genius" (*CW* 2:213). Both Goethe and Emerson consider man's ability to perceive nature as beauty to be a means of bringing him closer to grasping nature's ungraspable mystery. As we learn from the chapter on "Beauty" in *The Conduct of Life*: "The question of Beauty takes us out of surfaces to thinking of the foundations of things. Goethe said, 'The beautiful is a manifestation of secret laws of nature which, but for this appearance, had been forever concealed from us'" (*W* 6:288; *GA* 9:516).

How faithfully Emerson follows Goethe in matters aesthetic can be further illustrated with a passage from "The Eye and Ear," a lecture delivered on 27 December 1837:

> Art is vulgarly reckoned an imitation of nature and illusion is thought the highest success. . . . The great artist does not aim at imitation but at something higher. He proposes to show the mind of nature in the particular work he treats. He seeks not nature but the ideal which nature herself strives after. . . . As in nature abides everywhere quiet proportion and all relations enter without crowding into every particular product so must the work of art represent all nature within its little circuit. Therefore it is a maxim of Art that every true and perfect masterpiece is a whole; does take up into itself all beauty, and reminds the beholder of the entire beauty of nature. Hence follows the severe demand that the work of art should concentrate the look, the thought, the interest of the beholder so that he shall think of nothing out of it, nothing near, nothing else. A masterpiece of art should exclude and for the time annihilate everything else. (*EL* 2:266–67)

Emerson does not indicate Goethe's relevance to the aesthetic principles here enunciated, though he had Goethe clearly in mind when he first formulated them in his journal. For instance, on 2 November 1837, less than two months before he delivered the lecture on "The Eye and Ear," Emerson noted:

> I learn from my wise masters that Art does not love imitation . . . but proposes to show the Mind of Nature in the work. . . . Myron's Cow, according to Goethe, was so made as entirely to paint to the eye the beautiful instinct of the sucking calf & the sucked cow; and they mispraise it who say the herdman threw a stone at the cow to make her move.
>
> Goethe says "The mind & the endeavor of the Greeks is to deify man not to humanize the Godhead. Here is theomorphism not anthropomorphism. Moreover the Bestial should not be ennobled to the Human, but the Human of the Beast be raised, that so we may therein enjoy a higher pleasure of Art . . ."
>
> One more thought is that "the Artist concentrates the look, the thought,

the interest of the beholder, and he can think of nothing without, nothing near, nothing else; as truly a masterpiece of Art should exclude & for the time annihilate everything else." (*JMN* 5:416–17)

Every sentence in this journal entry is either a direct translation or a restatement of passages from Goethe's short essay "Myrons Kuh" ("Myron's Cow"; *GA* 13:637–46). In this essay Goethe argued that the ancients were wrong when they praised Myron's cow as a model of natural representation. He claimed that "it cannot possibly have been Myron's aim to present something so naturally as to have it confused with nature itself." Myron strove for "a higher sense . . . and certainly succeeded in differentiating *(abzusondern)* his works from nature" (*GA* 13:638). Still other Goethean ideas seem to have found their way into the passage I have quoted from the lecture "The Eye and Ear." Of special relevance is this statement from the *Italienische Reise:* "As in an organism of nature, so also in a work of art does life manifest itself in its completeness within the narrowest limits" (*GA* 11:503). Also important is a statement that Emerson translated from one of Goethe's botanical essays in October 1836: "Art ever represents itself entire in every single Art work" (*JMN* 5:224; *GA* 17:184).

Vivian C. Hopkins has said that Goethe opened "Emerson's eyes to form in sculpture and architecture" and that he also aroused "in his young follower a speculative interest in the form of art."[11] In his speculations on form Emerson remained close to his mentor. Both men recognize that *formally* works of art are inferior to works of nature. Works of nature have a formal integrity and authenticity for the most part lacking in works of art because the latter attain "perfection" only in the artist's *idea.* "The smallest production of nature," Emerson writes, quoting Goethe, "has the circle of its completeness within itself. . . . A work of art, on the other hand, has its completeness out of itself. The Best lies in the idea of the artist which he seldom or never reaches." Moreover, Emerson continues quoting, whereas "works of nature are ever a freshly uttered Word of God," there is "much that is traditional" in works of art (*EL* 1:72; *GA* 19:45). Objecting to the preponderance of tradition and convention in art, both Goethe and Emerson distinguish between "external form" and "inner form." The inner form, Goethe says, "cannot be grasped with hands; it can only be intuited" (*GA* 13:47–48). Inner form results from the artist's genius being able fully to apprehend the expres-

11. Hopkins, "Influence of Goethe," 328.

sive potential inherent in a given subject matter and to give it uniquely appropriate expression through his art. Inner form thus is the core and source of all genuine artistic forms, but few are the artists that can grasp it. As we learn from one of the *Maximen*, "Subject matter is available to everyone, substance is accessible only to those more germanely involved, and form remains a mystery to most" (*GA* 9:530).[12] It is only through his grasp and expression of inner form that the artist is capable of transcending tradition and convention. The artist "should avail himself of external influences only insofar as they further his development"; he should draw both "substance and form from the depths of his own being [and] impose his vision upon the subject matter" (*GA* 16:243). Emerson agreed: "The soul created the arts wherever they have flourished. It was in his own mind that the artist sought his model. It was an application of his own thought to the thing to be done and the conditions to be observed" (*CW* 2:47).

Donald MacRae has remarked that, unlike most of his fellow Romantics, Emerson preferred sculpture to painting and, in painting, delineation to color.[13] These preferences resulted, I think, from Emerson's sense that sculpture and drawing gave clearer expression to inner form than did color. Though Goethe never sided with either group in the contemporary sculpture-versus-painting debate, he commented in such loving detail upon both arts that proponents of either could claim him as a kindred spirit. Emerson, for one, derived support from Goethe's remarks connecting sculpture and design with "inner form." As part of his argument in "The Eye and Ear," for instance, he again quotes from Goethe: "In design . . . the soul seems to give utterance to her inmost being, and the highest mysteries of creation are precisely those which as far as relates to their ground plan rest entirely on design and modelling; these are the language in which she reveals them" (*EL* 2:265; *GA* 22:558). Emerson's enthusiasm for this Goethean idea becomes obvious when he adds: "This is one of the most valuable lessons we learn from collections of sculpture and paintings" (*EL* 2:265).

Neither Goethe nor Emerson believed, however, that art ever succeeded in completely expressing inner form. In Goethe's words, "every artistic form, even the most deeply felt one [*die gefühlteste*], has some untruth about it" (*GA* 13:48). Emerson also recognized that, even at its best, artistic form could not render "the immeasurable and divine" (*W*

---

12. For Goethe and inner form, see Reinhold Schwinger, "Innere Form."
13. Donald MacRae, "Emerson and the Arts," 81.

6:305). At the same time, Emerson understood as clearly as Goethe that the more closely art approaches the expression of inner form, the more it will partake of the "immeasurable and divine." He loved to quote a phrase which Goethe had borrowed from the humanist poet Johannes Secundus (Jan Everaerts, 1511–1536) and made his own: *vis superba formae* (the haughty power of form).[14] He stressed the incommensurability of that "haughty power," as when he asserted that "no laws of line or surface can ever account for the inexhaustible expressiveness of form" and that "the secret power of form over the imagination and affections transcends all our philosophy" (*W* 7:127). Both authors trace much of that "inexhaustible expressiveness" to the fluidity of form. In art, as in nature, the highest activity is "form-ing" (*Gestaltung*); in art "we do not encounter something completed, but something infinite that is ever in motion" (*GA* 19:566; 13:436). For Emerson also, "Beauty is the moment of transition, as if the form were just ready to flow into other forms" (*W* 6:292). In art, as in nature, the power of form resides in its infinite capacity for metamorphosis: "Nothing is so fleeting as form; yet never does it quite deny itself" (*CW* 2:8). It can, however, point beyond itself. In great sculpture, "the god or hero . . . is always represented in a transition *from* that which is representable to the senses, *to* that which is not." This state of transition has important critical implications: "The statue is then beautiful, when it begins to be incomprehensible" (*CW* 2:105).

Such speculations eventually carried Emerson beyond Goethe—and beyond art. Emerson agreed with Goethe that, as he put it in his lecture on Michelangelo (1835), "Man is the highest and indeed but the only proper object of plastic art" (*EL* 1:103; this statement is actually a translation from Goethe: see *GA* 13:142 and *JMN* 5:130). He further agreed that "we have in sculpture and in painting now in the world more noble form than the eye ever saw in actual nature," a statement he supports with a long quotation from the *Italienische Reise* (*EL* 2:265; *GA* 11:597–98). Ultimately, however, Emerson's commitment to nature made him impatient with even the highest forms of art. While granting that "picture and sculpture are the celebrations and festivities of form," he faulted even the greatest art for its inability to meet his demand for absolute formal fluidity. "True art is *never* fixed, but *always* flowing. . . . All works of art should not be detached, but extempore performances. A great man is a new statue in every attitude and action"

14. See *GA* 9:538; *W* 6:305; *JMN* 6:201; 9:16; 14:361.

(CW 2:216; my italics). Emerson exalted "the eternal picture which nature paints in the street with moving men and children, beggars, and fine ladies, draped in red, and green, and blue, and gray; long-haired, grizzled, white-faced, black-faced, wrinkled, giant, dwarf, expanded, elfish,—capped and based by heaven, earth, and sea" (CW 2:212). As we saw near the beginning of this chapter, Emerson credited Goethe with having penetrated "every secret of the Fine Arts" and with having "defined Art, its scope and laws." It may have seemed to Emerson that the only significant contribution left for him to make to the theory of art was to point beyond art. "A true announcement of the law of creation," Emerson wrote, "would carry art up into the kingdom of nature, and destroy its separate and contrasted existence" (CW 2:217).

CHAPTER 5

LITERATURE

Emerson's genius found expression in literature, not in art. Though he developed a considerable theoretical interest in art, he was bound to regard it as secondary to his interest in literature, the field that gave scope to his creative endeavors. Moreover, literary achievement and the experience that came with it enabled Emerson to speak on literary matters with a degree of authority unattainable to him on the subject of art. Remaining very much the novice in art, he was willing to be guided by someone he considered so eminent an expert as Goethe. In literature, however, armed with principles and insights that had stood the test of his own creative experience, Emerson was much more insistent on *his* point of view, on *his* values, and consequently was less willing to follow the guidance of anyone, no matter how prominent.

The fact remains, nevertheless, that Emerson considered Goethe the preeminent figure in modern literature and the writer whose achievement most clearly defined modernity in literature. Emerson did not hesitate, therefore, to draw support for his own aspirations to literary modernity from Goethe. Neither did he hesitate, however, to criticize Goethe the writer severely when he found him wanting by Emersonian standards. But whether he praised or blamed Goethe, whether he learned from him or rejected him, Emerson kept pointing to Goethe's modernity. Goethe's very defects were the defects of the modern writer *qua* modern writer. They were, in Emerson's view, the defects of the modern age, of which Goethe was the supreme literary embodiment.

Emerson derived from his confrontations with Goethe's oeuvre several important theoretical insights. In addition, Goethe contributed significantly to Emerson's appreciation of the importance of fact and actuality in literature. Finally, as a poet Emerson learned much from Goethe's practice in a particular poetic mode.

I

Goethe's most important contribution to modern thinking about literature was his theory of the symbol. Scholars widely divergent in interests and theoretical orientation have been unanimous in granting

Goethe pride of place in the development of the modern concept of symbolism. According to René Wellek, Goethe was "the first to draw the distinction between symbol and allegory in the modern way." Tzvetan Todorov also recognizes Goethe's priority in this matter; he credits Goethe with having introduced "the opposition between symbol and allegory." William K. Wimsatt and Cleanth Brooks advance the same view in their authoritative *Literary Criticism: A Short History*. Commenting on the concept of symbol (*Symbolbegriff*), Ernst Cassirer observes that Goethe "represents . . . most clearly the decisive turning point in modern consciousness." Hans-Georg Gadamer, examining the significance of symbol for his theory of hermeneutics, attributes to Goethe a "remolding (*Neuprägung*) of the concept of symbol." Hans Eichner, to cite one more authority, finds in Goethe and the circle of friends he inspired "the earliest lucid and comprehensive statements of the symbolic nature of art."[1]

Symbolism, to be sure, is omnipresent in Romantic literature, and in the speculative ferment of the age many thinkers on the subject may have reached similar conclusions independently. It would be unwise to claim, therefore, that similarities between Emerson's and Goethe's interpretations of the symbol are necessarily due to Goethe's influence or inspiration. Emerson may have been inspired by others; he may have developed important insights on his own. It remains true, nevertheless, that Goethe's far-reaching and profound speculations on the symbol seem to have been the ultimate source, whether directly or not, of all Romantic theorizing on the subject. In René Wellek's words:

> After [Goethe] many German aestheticians—Schelling, the Schlegels, Hegel, and others—elaborated, sometimes with a different terminology, the distinc-

1. Wellek, *History of Modern Criticism*, 1:210; Tzvetan Todorov, *Theories of the Symbol*, 200; William K. Wimsatt, Jr., and Cleanth Brooks, *Literary Criticism: A Short History*, 375; Ernst Cassirer, *Wesen und Wirkung des Symbolbegriffs*, 175; Hans-Georg Gadamer, *Wahrheit und Methode: Grundzüge einer philosophischen Hermeneutik*, 71–72; Eichner, "The Rise of Modern Science and the Genesis of Romanticism," 28 n. 36.

Todorov points out that the first writer "to have publicly contrasted symbol and allegory" was Goethe's friend Heinrich Meyer, in an essay "apparently inspired by the discussions he was having with Goethe" (*Über die Gegenstände der bildenden Kunst*, 1797). But Todorov adds: "We can understand why Meyer did not play an essential role in the history of these two concepts: he used the words quite uncritically, and he made no effort to specify exactly where the difference between them lay" (*Theories of the Symbol*, 212–13).

tion between allegory and symbol. . . . The concept of symbol penetrated almost everywhere: Coleridge picked it up from Goethe, the Schlegels, and Schelling; so did Carlyle; and their version of symbolism . . . became most important for Emerson and Poe.[2]

There is evidence, moreover, of Emerson's direct interest in Goethe's theory of the symbol. Vivian C. Hopkins has shown that Emerson adopted Goethean views on the subject while in Italy in 1833 and that he later gradually defined his own position through partial disagreement with Goethe's.[3] In some ways the mature Emerson's version of symbolism is indeed markedly different from Goethe's. Goethe would never have accepted Emerson's sweeping pansymbolism ("We are symbols, and inhabit symbols"; *CW* 3:12)[4] or Emerson's tendency to make the symbol disappear into the spiritual fact it represents ("the poet turns the world to glass"; *CW* 3:12). For Goethe the symbol maintains its concrete identity while suggesting the idea: the symbol is "the thing itself, without being the thing, and yet the thing" (*die Sache, ohne die Sache zu sein, und doch die Sache*).[5] It is through this very concreteness, as Gadamer has stressed, that the idea achieves reality in Goethe's mind. True symbolism occurs "where the particular represents the more general, not as a dream or shadow, but as a living, instantaneous [*lebendig-augenblickliche*] revelation of the inscrutable" (*GA* 9:532). Hopkins aptly summarizes the difference between Goethe and Emerson on this point: "For Goethe's theory of a symbol in which matter and spirit were perfectly balanced, Emerson substituted an artistic unit in which spirit dominated matter. In Emerson's theory, the most successful symbol would leave with the observer a dominant impression of spirit, independent of material shape, color, or sound."[6]

This difference in approach explains why Emerson, in contrast with Goethe, often appears to create symbols and use them with the utmost facility. Whereas Goethe's symbols remain opaque ("Symbolism changes . . . the idea into an image in such a way that the idea always remains infinitely active and unattainable in the image, and would remain inex-

2. René Wellek, *Discriminations: Further Concepts of Criticism*, 139.

3. Hopkins, "Influence of Goethe," 332–34.

4. On Goethe's avoidance of pansymbolism (*Pansymbolik*), see Eichhorn, *Idee und Erfahrung*, 135.

5. From "Nachträgliches zu 'Philostrats Gemälde,'" quoted in Eichhorn, *Idee und Erfahrung*, 133.

6. Gadamer, *Wahrheit und Methode*, 73; Hopkins, "Influence of Goethe," 333.

pressible even though expressed in all languages"; *GA* 9:639), Emerson's are transparent ("A happy symbol is a sort of evidence that your thought is just"; *W* 8:13). Unlike Goethe's, Emerson's symbols are also infinitely transferable: "The central identity enables any one symbol to express successively all the qualities and shades of real being. In the transmission of the heavenly waters, every hose fits every hydrant" (*CW* 4:68). Emerson, as Charles Feidelson has said, "embodied the monistic phase of symbolism, the sweeping sense of poetic fusion." This sense of fusion also appears in Emerson's claim in "History": "I can symbolize my thought by using the name of any creature, of any fact, because every creature is man agent or patient" (*CW* 2:18). Such a concept of symbolism, Feidelson points out, often emerges in Emerson's poetry as "the easy assumption that any image will do." While Lawrence Buell is right in stressing that "the core of Emerson's poetic is the idea of the symbolic image," in Emerson's poetic practice such images often appear rather rarefied.[7]

What more than anything else determined the nature of Emerson's symbolism, in theory and in practice, was his refusal ultimately to distinguish between the thinker and the poet: "The true philosopher and the true poet are one, and a beauty, which is truth, and a truth, which is beauty, is the aim of both" (*CW* 1:34). Such an identification resulted in a certain remoteness on Emerson's part "from the specific possibilities of the *literary* symbol."[8] This is all the more true because the identification usually is not so "balanced" as the passage just quoted from Emerson might suggest. Frequently the thinker goes far towards absorbing the poet's function. Emerson, to be sure, says that "poetry, if perfected, is the only verity; is the speech of man after the real, and not after the apparent" (*W* 8:20). The limitation "if perfected" recalls his statement in "The Poet": "I look in vain for the poet whom I describe" (*CW* 3:21). In any case, the perfection poetry should aim for is of a "philosophical" rather than a "poetical" nature: "Poetry is the perpetual endeavor to express the spirit of the thing, to pass the brute body and search the life and reason which causes it to exist;—to see that the object is always flowing away, whilst the spirit or necessity which causes it subsists" (*W* 8:17). The closer the poet approximates the thinker, the higher the value he has for Emerson. Whereas poets "live . . . to the beauty of the symbol," wise

7. Charles Feidelson, Jr., *Symbolism and American Literature*, 120, 123; Lawrence Buell, *Literary Transcendentalism: Style and Vision in the American Renaissance*, 153.
    8. Feidelson, *Symbolism and American Literature*, 122.

men, Emerson says, "live above the beauty of the symbol, to the beauty of the thing signified." The latter have "spiritual perception," while the former have merely "taste" (*JMN* 5:326). Statements like these call to mind Hegel's claim that art no longer satisfies the deepest needs of the spirit. They also remind us that Edmond Schérer's complaint about some of Goethe's later works is equally relevant to much of Emerson's poetic practice. Schérer pointed to the eclipse of the poet in works that are "wanting in the vigorous sensuousness, the concrete and immediate impression of things, which makes the artist, and which distinguishes him from the thinker."[9]

Emerson, moreover, is not always so much at variance with the Goethean theory of symbolism as the differences I have indicated might suggest. Sometimes he insists as emphatically as Goethe on the concreteness of the literary symbol and hence on the distinction between art and thought. As we learn from *Representative Men*: "Art expresses the one or the same by the different. Thought seeks to know unity in unity; poetry to show it by variety, that is, always by an object or symbol" (*CW* 4:32). While for Emerson it remains true that poetry derives its power from "the perception of the symbolic character of things, and the treating them as representative," he also recognizes that such symbolism and representativeness achieve poetic substantiality only through "a magnetic tenaciousness of an image, and by the treatment demonstrating that this pigment of thought is as palpable and objective to the poet as is the ground on which he stands, or the walls of houses about him" (*W* 8:27). Another similarity involves what Maurice Marache, in his magisterial *Le Symbole dans la pensée et l'oeuvre de Goethe*, has shown to have been a central preoccupation of Goethe's: raising vulgar reality to the level of poetry by turning it into symbol.[10] Emerson also insists that

> the distinctions which we make in events, and in affairs, of low and high, honest and base, disappear when nature is used as a symbol. Thought makes everything fit for use. The vocabulary of an omniscient man would embrace words and images excluded from polite conversation. What would be base, or even obscene, to the obscene, becomes illustrious, spoken in a new connexion of thought. . . . Small and mean things serve as well as great symbols. The meaner the type by which a law is expressed, the more pungent it is, and the more lasting in the memories of men. (*CW* 3:10–11)

9. Hegel, *Vorlesungen über die Aesthetik*, in *Sämtliche Werke*, 12:150–51; Edmond Schérer, quoted in Matthew Arnold, "A French Critic on Goethe," *Complete Prose Works*, 8:268.

10. Marache, *Le Symbole dans la pensée et l'oeuvre de Goethe*, 123.

Finally, as will be shown in the next chapter, Goethe's theory of the symbol also played an important part in Emerson's thinking on history and biography.

The relative independence from Goethe which Emerson displayed in his approach to symbol is absent from his responses to some of the other questions facing the modern writer. When in his lecture on "Art and Criticism" (1859) Emerson addressed himself to "a principal question in criticism in recent times—the Classic and Romantic, or what is classic?" his answer was entirely Goethean: "Classic art is the art of necessity; organic; modern or romantic bears the stamp of caprice or chance. . . . The classic unfolds, the romantic adds. The classic *should*, the modern *would*. The classic is healthy, the romantic is sick" (*W* 12:303–4). All of these definitions except the last are derived from Goethe's famous essay "Shakespeare und kein Ende" (*GA* 14:755–69, especially section ii); the last is taken from one of Goethe's conversations with Eckermann (*GA* 24:332). Journal entries show that Emerson was aware of these Goethean speculations long before "Art and Criticism." In 1836 he noted, for instance: "'*Should*' says Goethe 'was the genius of the Antique drama; *Would* of the Modern, but *should* is always great & stern; *would* is weak & small'" (*JMN* 5:200; *GA* 14:760–62). Emerson further follows Goethe in claiming that "antique" and "modern" are categories transcending time. As he says in "Art and Criticism," "there is anything but time in my idea of the antique. A clear or natural expression by word or deed is that which we mean when we love and praise the antique" (*W* 12:304–5; taken from an 1840 journal entry: *JMN* 7:505). In the aforementioned conversation with Eckermann, Goethe added: "Most recent works are romantic, not because they are recent, but because they are weak, morbid, and sick; and the works of antiquity are classical, not because they are ancient, but because they are strong, fresh, joyful, and healthy" (*GA* 24:332). In a similar vein, Goethe points out that Shakespeare, chronology notwithstanding, is in several respects "classical" (*GA* 14:759, 763; 13:842).

Goethe helped Emerson achieve insight into another important characteristic of modern literature. In a journal entry tentatively assigned to 1834 by Emerson's editors, Emerson quoted from *Winckelmann und sein Jahrhundert*: "'What happened interested them (the Greeks), what is thought & felt, us.' *Goethe*" (*JMN* 6:398; *GA* 13:417). Emerson appreciated this insight so much that he copied it again in 1861 (*JMN* 15:129). He also found a more elaborate version of this distinction between ancients and moderns in the *Italienische Reise*: "*They* represented reality, *we* usually its effect; *they* described the terrible, *we* describe terribly; *they* agreeable things, *we* agreeably, and so on" (*GA* 11:352). In such passages Goethe stresses the self-consciousness, the reflexivity of modern literature; and Emerson, recognizing these characteristics as central to modern literature, repeatedly echoes also this Goethean formulation of the ancient-modern dichotomy, as in this passage from "History" (1841) based upon journal entries of 1836 (*JMN* 5:198–99, 244):

> The costly charm of the ancient tragedy and indeed of all the old literature is, that the persons speak simply,—speak as persons who have great good sense without knowing it, before yet the reflective habit has become the predominant habit of the mind. Our admiration of the antique is not admiration of the old, but of the natural. The Greeks are not reflective, but perfect in their senses and in their health, with the finest physical organization in the world. (*CW* 2:15)

This cultural typology also informs Emerson's definition of the modern age in *The American Scholar*: it is "the Reflective or Philosophical age . . . the age of Introversion." In the modern age, we "are critical. We are embarrassed with second thoughts. We cannot enjoy any thing for hankering to know whereof the pleasure consists. We are lined with eyes. We see with our feet" (*CW* 1:66).

In Emerson's view, Goethe not only interpreted but also exemplified these modern characteristics. He describes Goethe as "Argus-eyed," as "seem[ing] to see out of every pore of his skin" (*CW* 4:156, 157). Goethe, "the all-knowing poet" (*W* 7:323), perhaps "knew too much": his sight was "microscopic" to the point that it interfered with his art (*CW* 4:165). Still, the "reflective and critical wisdom" informing *Faust*, for example, "makes the poem more truly the flower of this time" (*CW* 4:157). In his late retrospective "Historic Notes of Life and Letters in New England," Emerson restated his conviction that *Faust* was "the most remarkable literary work of the age" because it embodied modern introversion (*W* 10:328). Though Emerson was sometimes severely critical of *Faust*, he never denied its being the preeminent modern poem. His harshest criticism appears, not surprisingly, in the section on "Morals" in "Poetry and Imagination," but even there *Faust* is considered to be the representative poem of the age, the poem that "stands unhappily related to the whole modern world" (*W* 8:69). Emerson expresses his love-hate attitude toward *Faust* most tersely in "The Man of Letters": "The great poem of the age is the disagreeable poem of Faust" (*W* 10:245).

Emerson's commitment to literary modernity is further illustrated by his preferring *Faust*, despite all his objections to it, to Goethe's most "perfect" play, *Iphigenie*. Emerson is aware of *Iphigenie*'s exquisiteness, but as he sees it, the play suffers from a flaw more fatal than any that detract from the greatness of *Faust*: instead of being truly modern, it is merely a "modern antique" (*JMN* 8:400). *Iphigenie* is "a pleasing, moving, even heroic work yet with the great deduction of being an imitation of the antique. How can a great genius endure to make paste-jewels?" (*JMN* 5:148). The fact that Goethe turned to a Euripidean model apparently blinded Emerson to *Iphigenie*'s essential modernity. Schiller, whose credentials as a student of Greek literature and of drama far outweigh Emerson's, said of *Iphigenie*: "It is . . . so astonishingly modern and un-Greek that I cannot understand how it was ever thought to resemble a Greek play."[11] Later scholars have illustrated and amplified Schiller's statement voluminously. One of the ways in which *Iphigenie* is modern consists precisely in that interiorization of fate which Emerson recognized and praised in *Torquato Tasso*: "crises ought . . . to grow out of the faults & the conditions of the parties; as in Goethe's Tasso" (*JMN* 7:464).

Such interiorization also characterizes the modern novel, whose chief exemplar, in Emerson's view, was once again Goethe. Emerson dismissed most novels as "novels of costume or of circumstance." He appreciated only "novels of character," and "the best specimen" in this category he considered to be *Wilhelm Meister* (*W* 12:374–78). Goethe's achievement as a novelist was such that *Wilhelm Meister* was, in fact, "the first of its kind." Its merits were legion: "so new, so provoking to the mind, gratifying it with so many and so solid thoughts, just insights into life and manners and characters; so many good hints for the conduct of life, so many unexpected glimpses into a higher sphere, and never a trace of rhetoric or dulness" (*CW* 4:160). The novel certainly has its flaws, Emerson admits, referring to what he regards as its too frank realism, yet "the book remains ever so new and unexhausted, that we must even let it go its way, and be willing to get what good from it we can, assured that it has only begun its office, and has millions of readers yet to serve" (*CW* 4:161). Emerson here takes a long-range view of Goethe's influence, as Carlyle did when he said that it might well take more than a thousand years for Goethe's impact to be fully felt.[12] What confers on a book like

11. Quoted in Lewes, *Life and Works of Goethe*, 272.
12. For Carlyle, see Leonard A. Willoughby, "The Living Goethe" 9. For a general

Wilhelm Meister lasting greatness, according to Emerson, is Goethe's "habitual reference to interior truth" (*CW* 4:161).

Characteristics such as reflexivity, introversion, and interiorization are obviously aspects of subjectiveness, which Emerson considered both the glory and the curse of modern literature. It is impossible, however, to appreciate fully Emerson's ambivalence without examining Goethe's complex understanding of subjectivity in literature.

II

On no literary question does Emerson in his journals quote or refer to Goethe more conscientiously than on the respective roles of "subjective" and "objective." Not only was this a question centrally relevant to Emerson, but also one on which Goethe's remarks are so fascinating that few of his readers have been able to resist quoting and examining them. Goethe said that all his works were but "fragments of a great confession" (*Bruchstücke einer großen Konfession*; *GA* 10:312) and that *Werther* was "a creature . . . which [he] had fed, like a pelican, with the blood of [his] own heart" (*GA* 24:545). In an important self-assessment, Goethe claimed that he had liberated the new generation of poets precisely by teaching them that "the artist must work from within, that, do what he will, he can express only his individuality" (*GA* 14:398).

Nevertheless, Goethe is not an apostle of subjectivity. Even calling his works "fragments of a great confession" does not, in context, support the notion that Goethe regarded his works as merely subjective. What he does say is that it was his lifelong tendency to *objectify* his joys and sorrows, to *transmute* them into images and poems (*GA* 10:311–12). True, the poet "can express only his individuality," but the great poet does so by finding in the world appropriate objects and facts that not only enable him to express his inner self, but also allow that inner self to grow and achieve fuller consciousness. Hence the greater the creative potential of the inner self, the greater the demands the true poet will make upon the world. Somewhat paradoxically, he will express the world in the process of expressing himself. Shakespeare is so great a poet, Goethe argued, "because hardly anyone else observed the world as he did, because hardly anyone else, in the act of expressing his inner perceptions, provides the reader in the same degree with an awareness of the world" (*GA* 14:756). Shakespeare was far removed from the self-

---

discussion of Emerson's attitude toward fiction, see Jeffrey Steinbrink, "Novels of Circumstance and Novels of Character: Emerson's View of Fiction."

absorbed subjectivity that Goethe condemned as "the general disease of the present age" (*GA* 24:170).

Emerson fully approved of Goethe's stance. Quoting from one of Goethe's conversations with Eckermann, he noted in an 1837–1838 journal:

> All Epochs considered in their receding & dissolution are subjective; but on the contrary all advancing Epochs have an objective direction. Our whole present Epoch is a receding since it is a subjective period. This you see not only in poetry but also in painting & many other things. Every great Effort, on the other hand, tends from within out upon the world. (*JMN* 5:313; *GA* 24:172)

In Emerson's view, Goethe ranked with Shakespeare as a poet capable of grasping creatively the inwardness of the "wholly other." He recognized as early as April 1835 that "the true genius the Shakspear & Goethe sees the tree & sky & man as they are, enters into them whilst the inferior writer dwells evermore with himself" (*JMN* 5:27). Unlike authors such as Tieck and Richter, who are "introversive to a fault," Goethe, "the truest of all writers . . . writes of real Man . . . of what has been lived" (*JMN* 5:202). The important criterion here is what Goethe called, in the first passage quoted in this paragraph, the "objective direction" (*objektive Richtung*), a criterion that will dominate Emerson's theory in "Thoughts on Modern Literature."

In this important essay Emerson distinguishes between two kinds of subjectiveness. The first—the good kind—is "founded on that insatiable demand for unity, the need to recognize one nature in all the variety of objects, which always characterizes a genius of the first order" (*W* 12:313). The second—"vicious subjectiveness"—is a mode of "intellectual selfishness" that refers everything to self (*W* 12:314). Emerson then points to the source of this distinction:

> The criterion which discriminates these two habits in the poet's mind is the tendency of his composition; namely, whether it leads us to Nature, or to the person of the writer. The great always introduce us to facts; small men introduce us always to themselves. The great man, even whilst he relates a private fact personal to him, is really leading us away from him to an universal experience. His own affection is in Nature, in *what is*, and, of course, all his communication leads outward to it, starting from whatsoever point. (*W* 12:314–15)

The foremost exemplar of this "objective tendency," Emerson believed, was Goethe, that "resolute realist" who was determined "to see things for what they are." Reading him gives one the impression that "there was never an observer before." His "deep realism" enabled him to grasp the soul of "every fact he treats," to grasp the "eternal reason why it was so, and not otherwise" (W 12:323, 324). Emerson admits, of course, that Goethe was sometimes infected by the "vicious subjectiveness" of the age, but he is careful to point out that whereas "this subtle element of egotism" lowers Goethe's "moral influence," it "certainly does not seem to deform his compositions" (W 12:326).

The most important practical result of Goethe's example in this matter was Emerson's developing a greater respect for objectivity, for the actual, for the fact. The true poet, Emerson says, "describes every object with a delight in the thing itself. . . . [He] throws his spirit into whatever he contemplates and enjoys the making it speak that it would say" (EL 1:272-73). A statement like this should not be dismissed because it seems so greatly at variance with Emerson's more habitual, more purely "idealistic" view of poetry. It suggests an antithesis in his thinking on poetry, which, like so much of his thinking on any subject, is all the richer for its dialectical tensions. Goethe's influence here, as elsewhere in Emerson, was "antithetical" in tending toward a validation of the concrete, of the actual. A fact, Emerson can say in this phase of his dialectic, "is true poetry, and the most beautiful of fables" (CW 1:44). Fact surpasses fiction because fact contains essential reality; indeed, the fact contains so much of the essence of reality that it remains forever beyond our grasp: "Fact is better than fiction, if only we could get pure fact" (W 7:107). In his journal Emerson copied Johann Heinrich Merck's remark, which Goethe quoted with approval in Dichtung und Wahrheit because it went far to explain the nature of his achievement, that it was Goethe's "unchangeable tendency . . . to idealize the actual" instead of "realiz-[ing] the imaginary" (JMN 6:174; GA 10:787). For Goethe, true "idealizing" meant attempting to grasp and express the spirit of the actual, which was exactly what Emerson advocated in The American Scholar: "What would we really know the meaning of? The meal in the firkin; the milk in the pan; the ballad in the street; the news of the boat; the glance of the eye; the form and the gait of the body;—show me the ultimate reason of these matters;—show me the sublime presence of the highest spiritual cause lurking, as always it does lurk, in these suburbs and extremities of nature" (CW 1:67-68).

Such theories have, of course, stylistic implications. Over and over again Emerson praised the concreteness and substantiality of Goethe's style. As early as 1834 he wrote: "Goethe was a person who hated words that did not stand for things" (*JMN* 4:301). He praised Goethe's "impatience of words" two years later: "To read Goethe is an economy of time; for you shall find no word that does not stand for a thing" (*JMN* 5:133). He traced the phantasmagoria in *Faust, Part Two* to "the same desire that every word should be a thing" (*CW* 2:19; cf. *JMN* 5:315). This substantiality explains why in so voluminous a work as *Wilhelm Meister* there is "never a trace of rhetoric or dulness"; in fact, it contains "not a word too much" (*CW* 4:160, 161). Far from tending to embellishment and verbosity, Goethe's writings are models of simplicity and conciseness: "He writes in the plainest and lowest tone, omitting a great deal more than he writes, and putting ever a thing for a word" (*CW* 4:158). Goethe always preferred "common expressions" (*JMN* 5:316). He prided himself "not on his learning or eccentric flights, but that he knew how to write German. And many of his poems are so idiomatic, so strongly rooted in the German soil, that they are the terror of translators" (*W* 12:284). Emerson, as already indicated, also considered Goethe "the most modern of the moderns" in his "perception of the worth of the vulgar"—a perception that enables man to see "that things near are not less beautiful and wondrous than things remote" (*CW* 1:68). Goethe had complained to Eckermann that "few people have imagination for the truth of reality [*eine Phantasie für die Wahrheit des Realen*]." Instead, most people prefer to contemplate "strange countries and conditions of which they know nothing and to which their imagination can give forms sufficiently odd" (*GA* 24:166). Emerson seems to echo this complaint when, in *The American Scholar*, he criticizes those neglecting "the common" in favor of "long journeys into far countries." Emerson's literary program is entirely in Goethe's spirit: "I ask not for . . . what is doing in Italy or Arabia . . . I embrace the common, I explore and sit at the feet of the familiar, the low" (*CW* 1:67).

Many influential voices have supported Emerson's perception that Goethe's was an utterly modern style, a style suited to the realities of modern life and the requirements of modern literature. Novalis stressed the "anti-poetic" quality of Goethe's writing in *Wilhelm Meisters Lehrjahre*. He called the novel "a *Candide* directed against poetry," destructive of anything "romantic" or "mystical," in sum, a work "thoroughly *prosaic*—and modern" ("durchaus *prosaisch*—und modern"). Thomas Mann has celebrated the nimbleness, subtlety, and suppleness which endow Goethe's prose with its indescribable charm. His words, Mann says, always seem to be newly created and to remain ever fresh, while Goethe throughout speaks in a voice that is neither grand nor solemn nor pathetic, but thoroughly "average" (*mittler*), in a word, *prosaisch*. Georg Lukács has praised Goethe's prose for its avoidance of "spurious poetry," "sterile romanticism," and "rapturousness." Yet Lukács makes clear that the plasticity, pithiness, and subtlety of Goethe's style prevented him from becoming a mere prose "technician." Perhaps the contemporary West German novelist Martin Walser has best expressed the scope of Goethe's stylistic revolution: Goethe freed "our feelings and language from the rituals of court and church. . . . It is to his balking at any abstraction, to his insistence on vision, on what one feels, perceives, that we owe the awakening of the German language, numbed by the pretentious languages of church and state."[13] Emerson's relative lack of familiarity with German literature apart from Goethe did not allow him, unlike the writers just quoted, to appreciate Goethe's stylistic significance in its full historical context. But, if anything, this cultural disadvantage made Emerson's recognition of Goethe as a truly modern writer all the more remarkable.

Emerson's own stylistic values seem to be entirely in accord with Goethe's. He also advocates conciseness ("Spartans, stoics, heroes, saints and gods use a short and positive speech"; W 10:169), substance ("Literature is but a poor trick when it busies itself to make words pass for things"; EL 3:204), concreteness ("Wise men pierce this rotten diction and fasten words again to visible things"; CW 1:20), precision ("Language should aim to describe the fact. It is not enough to suggest it and magnify it"; W 10:164), and appreciation of the "vulgar" ("The low expression is strong and agreeable"; W 10:169). We certainly recognize in Emerson's practice as an essayist another characteristic of Goethe's, which Emerson remarked on in 1837: "Goethe prefers to drop a profound observation incidentally to stating it circumstantially" (JMN 5:317). It has to be admitted, however, that in suppleness and in that ineffable something called charm, Emerson's prose never equals Goethe's.

Sometimes, moreover, Emerson found Goethe a little too concrete, too realistic. The "actual men and women" in *Wilhelm Meister*, for example, are "even too faithfully painted" (W 12:330). By presenting men and women as they were and not as they ought to be, by preferring the "Actual" to the "Ideal," Goethe became "the poet of limitation, not of possibility; of this world, and not of religion and hope; in short . . . the

---

13. Novalis, *Schriften*, 3:638–39, 646; Mann, "Goethe als Repräsentant des bürgerlichen Zeitalters," in *Gesammelte Werke*, 9:312; Lukács, *Faust und Faustus*, 38, 45–46; Martin Walser, "Things Go Better With Goethe."

poet of prose, and not of poetry" (*W* 12:331). This criticism, from "Thoughts on Modern Literature" (1840), recurs in *Representative Men* (1850), where Emerson regards Goethe as embodying nineteenth-century culture so completely that he failed to ascend to "the highest grounds from which genius has spoken . . . [to] the highest unity . . . to the moral sentiment . . . to pure truth" (*CW* 4:163). Such statements have a certain validity, but they say little more than that Goethe was not a New England Transcendentalist. Emerson admits as much when, after having denied that Goethe gave voice to "the transcendent muse," he credits him with the supreme Emersonian virtue of being true to his own nature: "Yet in the court and law to which we ordinarily speak, and without adverting to absolute standards, we claim for him the praise of truth, of fidelity to his intellectual nature. . . . Let him have the praise of the love of truth" (*W* 12:327). Elsewhere Emerson is even more cautious in his criticism:

> If you criticise a fine genius, the odds are that you are out of your reckoning, and, instead of the poet, are censuring your own caricature of him. . . . After taxing Goethe as a courtier, artificial, unbelieving, worldly,—I took up this book of Helena [i.e., an episode in *Faust, Part Two*, published separately], and found him an Indian of the wilderness, a piece of pure nature like an apple or an oak, large as morning or night, and virtuous as a briar-rose. (*CW* 4:163)

Indeed, Emerson's admiration of *Faust, Part Two* was such that he called it "the grandest enterprise of literature that has been attempted since the Paradise Lost" (*JMN* 9:43).

Nevertheless, more often than not, Emerson remained deeply ambivalent about Goethe the poet. His criticism is sometimes surprising, as when he writes: "The great felicities, the miracles of poetry, he has never" (*W* 12:327); "This lawgiver of art is not an artist" (*CW* 4:165); or "He is . . . artistic, but not artist" (*CW* 4:163). Goethe wrote in many poetic modes, and often he showed himself capable of the most exquisite lyricism. It is possible that Emerson had no ear for the music of Goethe's poetry. Neither, after all, did T. S. Eliot—at first. According to Eliot, Goethe merely "dabbled in . . . poetry and made no great success of [it]"; he should have stuck to his real talent, which, as Eliot saw it, was for writing polished maxims in the manner of La Rochefoucauld or Vauvenargues. It took Eliot many years to begin to realize that Goethe was indeed "a great lyric poet."[14] If an Eliot could for so long fail to

14. T. S. Eliot, *The Use of Poetry and the Use of Criticism*, 99; *On Poetry and Poets*, 264.

appreciate one of the greatest lyric poets in European literature, Emerson's similar failure is certainly understandable.

It seems clear, however, that ultimately Emerson refused to grant Goethe supreme status in poetry on the same ground that he denied him the highest achievement in prose: as poet of the "Actual," Goethe did not represent the ideal of the vatic poet that Emerson articulated in his essay "The Poet." Goethe was not the inspired poet, the "Redeemer of the human mind." Instead he was "content to fall into the track of vulgar poets and spend on common aims his splendid endowments" (W 12:332). Being such a poet, he was, of course, all the more representative of his age, in which there was "no poet, but scores of poetic writers" (CW 4:156). Among these, Goethe was the greatest by far: "Still he is a poet, poet of a prouder laurel than any contemporary . . . [he] strikes the harp with a hero's strength and grace" (CW 4:157). More than anyone else, Goethe "has clothed our modern existence with poetry" (CW 4:157):

> In newer days of war and trade,
> Romance forgot, and faith decayed,
> When Science armed and guided war,
> And clerks the Janus-gates unbar,
> When France, where poet never grew,
> Halved and dealt the globe anew,
> GOETHE, raised o'er joy and strife,
> Drew the firm lines of Fate and Life
> And brought Olympian wisdom down
> To court and mart, to gown and town.
> Stooping, his finger wrote in clay
> The open secret of to-day.
> (W 9:223)

III

In his major study, *New England Literary Culture: From Revolution Through Renaissance*, Lawrence Buell points out that though most New England poets were familiar with the work of a considerable number of their fellow New England poets, "in no case was any New England poet *the* primary demonstrable influence on another's work." Instead, "all the major figures of the period were nurtured more on European models than on American."[15] My concern, needless to say, is with Goethe's

15. Lawrence Buell, *New England Literary Culture: From Revolution Through Renaissance*, 135.

share in the European influence on Emerson as poet.

The limitations that Emerson perceived in Goethe the poet made him consider Goethe, as already indicated, all the more representative of the modern age. At the same time, some of these limitations made it easier for Emerson to recognize Goethe as a poet akin to the kind of poet he conceived himself to be, and consequently as a poet whose example was relevant to his own poetic endeavors. That Goethe, in Emerson's view, was incapable of the highest lyricism made him more, rather than less, approachable to one who wrote in his most famous self-definition as a poet: "My singing be sure is very 'husky,' & is for the most part in prose." Emerson did consider himself a true poet, but on rather different grounds: "Still am I a poet in the sense of a perceiver & dear lover of the harmonies that are in the soul & in matter, & specially of the correspondences between these & those" (L 1:435). There is more to Emerson's poetic achievement than these statements from 1835 suggest. They indicate, nevertheless, an essential truth about Emerson: he was basically, to quote Robert Frost, a "philosophical poet"[16] or—since "philosophical" might suggest poems like the *magna opera* of Dante and Lucretius, poems, that is, inspired by a unifying, all-pervasive metaphysic—at any rate, a poet of ideas. Emerson belongs, as Carl F. Strauch has said, "to that rarest class—the poets of ideas." It is not surprising, therefore, that Emerson, though insensitive to much of Goethe's finest poetry, readily appreciated the *Gedankenlyrik*—Goethe's poetry of ideas. In fact, it was "as a poet of ideas" rather than in any of his other literary incarnations that Goethe "probably most appealed to Emerson."[17]

Recognizing Emerson as a poet of ideas has implications for his status as a poet. The most thorough and impressive among recent indictments of Emerson as poet is David Porter's *Emerson and Literary Change*. As Porter sees it, Emerson's poetic practice "sacrifices art to meaning and experiential fullness to the goal of converting the world into idea." Emerson's poems "are designed for the understanding rather than for the more ambiguous currents of feelings. . . . Deliberately ascending above the teeming and distracting world, the poet insists upon an *understanding* of life and consequently upon a view from a distance." Emerson thus slighted "what poetry has known since Homer" and what Whitman and Dickinson remembered so well—that poetry's authentic mode of being involves concreteness and particularity. Porter's argument has consider-

---

16. Robert Frost, "On Emerson," 12.
17. Carl F. Strauch, "The Year of Emerson's Poetic Maturity: 1834," 353, 359.

able merit. It is true, of course, that poetry has generally lived by the concrete and the particular, and it is also true that Emerson's "occasional excursions into particularity tend to be innocuous."[18] But the unspoken assumption behind Porter's argument is that the *kind* of poetry that Emerson most often practiced, the poetry of ideas, is not an authentic poetic mode. True poetry of ideas may be rare, as Strauch suggests, but that seems all the more reason for us to approach it without bias, trying to judge it on its own merits and within the historically developed understandings that inform this genre.

Most of the poetry Goethe wrote in the course of his long career was not, strictly speaking, poetry of ideas. From about 1790 onward, however, he also produced a considerable body of *Gedankenlyrik* which Emerson, given his poetic tendencies and limitations, was better equipped to appreciate than Goethe's other poetry. The older Goethe often yearned for a poetry in which thought could be expressed "as it was" without being "disfigured" by figurative language, without the clouding interference of tropes (*eine Poesie ohne Tropen*). He wanted to express reality in a truer way than the imagination—which he had come to think of as a "vague, unreliable faculty" (*GA* 8:271)—was capable of providing. In line with this thinking is the rather startling claim in *Dichtung und Wahrheit* that the essence of a poem is what is left of the poem after it has been translated into prose (*GA* 10:540). Devotion to such ideals explains why so many of Goethe's later poems read like good, colloquial prose, or at any rate, like "rhymed prose."[19]

Such poetry has its virtues, however. It is forcefully conceptual, tightly argued, informed by polarity and thus given structure and meaning by the interdependence of implicit or explicit opposites. Though conceptual, such poetry is not abstract. Its concepts derive their force from their *growing out of* concrete experiences or from their having *absorbed* such experiences. To put it differently, the concepts are "experienced" concepts, that is, experienced by a poetic "I." What makes for poetry of ideas is the elevation of experience or of the emotion which experience evokes to, in Viëtor's words, "a sphere which lies above the concrete moment and the personal reference." In successful poetry of ideas, the concrete and the personal are *aufgehoben*, in the dual Hegelian sense of the term: they are transcended and yet preserved.[20] The ideas have absorbed and

18. David Porter, *Emerson and Literary Change*, 16–17.
19. See Fairley, *Study of Goethe*, 169–70; and Gundolf, *Goethe*, 667.
20. Viëtor, *Goethe the Poet*, 231; Hegel, *Phänomenologie des Geistes*, 90: "Das *Auf-*

are shaped by the experiences they transcend. The process of transforming experiences into ideas results in a dynamic poetry very different from
the static, didactic versification of moral or philosophical doctrines that
one finds so often in the eighteenth century. As for the role of polarity, in
poetry as elsewhere polarity was Goethe's way of keeping his thought
close to natural law and of maintaining order and coherence while
ranging far and wide, while striving to be as "comprehensive" as nature
herself. This characteristic of Goethe's poetry appealed to an Emerson
who deplored the fact that his own poems "did not contain sufficient
evidence of the 'polarity' of existence, of how its inevitable law is action
and reaction, of how every statement contains the seed of its opposite."[21]
Through poetry informed by polarity, Goethe could show Emerson how
to write poems that were, paradoxically, comprehensive through compression, that is, multifarious in their implications and yet centralized
through the interplay of opposites. Or, to put it differently, the interplay
of opposites itself suggested a dialectic of infinite implication and thus
led to a comprehensiveness of poetic "statement" at variance with the
restraint and compression of the language. This, to be sure, is a poetry
addressed to the understanding, but not therefore lacking in resonance
and scope, as Porter claims in relation to Emerson's poetry.[22]

Poetry of ideas is often epigrammatic in style. Goethe wrote several
collections of epigrams, the best-known being *Venetianische Epigramme*.
Moreover, an epigrammatic style pervades many of his poems of ideas
that are not, generically speaking, epigrams. Characteristic of his epigrams is that they are not merely intellectual statements but are shown to
grow out of experiences or perceptions. Thus, they are also rooted in a
larger world, and their antitheses grow out of the polarity inherent in
that world and in the totality of existence. Goethean epigrams, in other
words, often involve realms of awareness far beyond merely verbal
paradox or intellectual contradiction. They often confront idea with
event, or thought with perception, or wisdom with experience—the
second member of the confrontation linking the idea or the thought or

---

heben stellt seine wahrhafte gedoppelte Bedeutung dar . . . es ist ein *Negieren* und ein
Aufbewahren zugleich" (*Aufheben* represents a true dichotomy in meaning . . . it is
simultaneously a *canceling* and a *preserving*).

21. F. O. Matthiessen, *American Renaissance: Art and Expression in the Age of
Emerson and Whitman*, 63.

22. See Porter, *Emerson and Literary Change*, 19, 28–29.

the wisdom to the world of nature or history. As just one example, let us take *Venetianische Epigramme*, no. 53:

> Frankreichs traurig Geschick, die Großen mögens bedenken;
> Aber bedenken fürwahr sollen es Kleine noch mehr.
> Große gingen zugrunde: doch wer beschützte die Menge
> Gegen die Menge? Da war Menge der Menge Tyrann.
>
> (*GA* 1:233)

> (Let the great of the earth ponder the sad fate of France; but the common people should ponder it even more. Great ones perished: but who protected the masses from the masses? There the masses were tyrants to the masses.)

This richness of idea-engendering experience, explicit in many of Goethe's epigrams, is implicit in the epigrammatic style often characterizing his poems of ideas. Goethe's epigrammatic language in its simplicity and terseness is but experience transmuted and condensed.

Carl Strauch has carefully defined the character of Goethe's influence on Emerson as a poet. Examining four poems signaling Emerson's attainment of poetic maturity—"The Rhodora," "Xenophanes," "Each and All," and "The Snow-Storm"—Strauch concludes that while "the influence of Goethe is not specifically discernible" in any of them, "it is nonetheless great in its catalytic effect." Goethe provided "the generally pervasive inspiration for Emerson's own imaginative rendering of philosophic ideas."[23] Goethe's influence on Emerson's poetry of ideas, in other words, is one of method rather than of concepts. Having read Gérando, Cudworth, and Coleridge, Emerson had no need to turn to Goethe's "Eins und Alles" for the idea expressed in "Each and All." What "Eins und Alles" and similar Goethe poems could teach Emerson was *how* to write good poems of ideas.

That Emerson learned much from Goethe's example is evident also from poems other than the four for which Strauch has shown Goethe to have been a significant model. A case in point is "The Problem" (*W* 9:6–9). The poem opens with an experience involving the emotions and the aesthetic sense:

> I like a church; I like a cowl;
> I love a prophet of the soul;

---

23. Strauch, "Emerson's Poetic Maturity," 357, 358–59.

And on my heart monastic aisles
Fall like sweet strains, or pensive smiles;
Yet not for all his faith can see
Would I that cowled churchman be.

(1–6)

The second line goes beyond the first in intensifying the emotion (from "like" to "love") and transferring it to a beauty that is truth ("prophet of the soul") rather than a primarily aesthetic experience, as is the case in "church" and "cowl" as objects of "like" and in lines 3–4. Yet not even the "love" of line 2, the object of which is repeated in line 5 ("all his faith can see"), can induce the speaker to wish himself to be a "churchman."

In the opening lines of this 1839 poem, Emerson, the former clergyman, was obviously dramatizing a very personal experience, as is also evidenced by the prose "version" of the poem, dated 28 August 1838:

> It is very grateful to my feelings to go into a Roman Cathedral, yet I look as my countrymen do at the Roman priesthood. It is very grateful to me to go into an English Church & hear the liturgy read. Yet nothing would induce me to be the English priest. I find an unpleasant dilemma in this, nearer home. I dislike to be a clergyman & refuse to be one. Yet how rich a music would be to me a holy clergyman in my town. It seems to me he cannot be a man, quite & whole. Yet how plain is the need of one, & how high, yes highest, is the function. Here is Division of labor that I like not. A man must sacrifice his manhood for the social good. Something is wrong, I see not what. (*JMN* 7:60)

The tension throughout and the lack of resolution at the end of this statement demonstrate the intensity and the continuity of Emerson's involvement in the question here presented. "The Problem" is but another product of that involvement, but a product that goes far beyond its prose analogue as stated in the journal.

The first six lines of "The Problem," as we have seen, express an experience that leaves the "I" with contradictory feelings. The "I" attempts to find a way out of the emotional antinomy by raising it to the level of thought and thus setting the stage for confronting it intellectually: "Why should the vest on him allure, / Which I could not on me endure?" (7–8). The poem answers this personal question by transcending the personal, by addressing itself to issues of universal significance. The churchman "attracts" because he is *one* of the expressions of universal Truth. Anyone wanting to remain receptive to *all* such expressions, however, cannot accept the identity (and its attendant limitations) that commitment to *one* expression of Truth would impose upon him. Though appreciative of a priestly "prophet of the soul," the speaker therefore refuses to *be* one: the commitment thereby entailed would preclude his receptivity to the myriad other ways in which Truth has expressed and is still expressing itself. Each of these expressions is as valuable as the churchman's:

> Not from a vain or shallow thought
> His awful Jove young Phidias brought;
> Never from lips of cunning fell
> The thrilling Delphic oracle;
> Out from the heart of nature rolled
> The burdens of the Bible old;
> The litanies of nations came,
> Like the volcano's tongue of flame,
> Up from the burning core below,—
> The canticles of love and woe:
> The hand that rounded Peter's dome
> And groined the aisles of Christian Rome
> Wrought in a sad sincerity;
> Himself from God he could not free;
> He builded better than he knew;—
> The conscious stone to beauty grew.
> (9–24)

This passage shows the speaker's conception of Truth to be a pantheistic one, a point further emphasized in the remaining sections of the poem, where Nature, Art, Thought, and Religion are all One. Like Nature, Art grows organically "out of Thought's interior sphere" (39):

> These temples grew as grows the grass;
> Art might obey, but not surpass.
> The passive Master lent his hand
> To the vast soul that o'er him planned.
> (45–48)

Religion is but one more expression of the One: "And the same power that reared the shrine / Bestrode the tribes that knelt within" (49–50). Such expression is ever-present and ever-new:

> The word by seers or sibyls told,
> In groves of oak, or fanes of gold,
> Still floats upon the morning wind,

Still whispers to the willing mind.
One accent of the Holy Ghost
The heedless world hath never lost.
                    (57–62)

Critics often regard the last ten lines of the poem (63–72) as a mere restatement of the opening.[24] It seems to me that the poem ends very differently from the way it begins. The opening lines express a problematic *feeling*, the emotionally unresolved experience of a problem. The end of the poem resolves the problem *intellectually*. The awareness of universal, ever-ongoing expression of truth, developed in lines 9 through 62, has led the speaker to the realization that any claim to exclusive truth is simply invalid. In the speaker's experience the chief such claimant is, of course, Christianity. Reinforced by the argument in 9–62, he now confidently rejects the greatest Christian authorities, while still appreciating them aesthetically, that is, the way he would appreciate Shakespeare, Michelangelo, Phidias, "the litanies of nations," "seers or sibyls," because like all of these or like any other expression of the One, Christianity, in its inspired moments, is inherently beautiful and to that extent true. By the end of the poem, the speaker has come to understand his "problem": he cannot *be* a churchman because of Christianity's traditional insistence on its *exclusive* possession of truth. Yet to the extent that Christianity indeed expresses an aspect of the One, he can love it. After the assertions in the passages already quoted, the speaker is ready to dismiss any monopolistic claims to truth:

I know what say the fathers wise,—
The Book itself before me lies,
Old *Chrysostom*, best Augustine,
And he who blent both in his line,
The younger *Golden Lips* or mines,
Taylor, the Shakespeare of divines.
His words are music in my ear,
I see his cowled portrait dear;
And yet, for all his faith could see,
I would not the good bishop be.
                    (63–72)

"The Problem" is a poem of ideas, but as in Goethe's similar poems,

---

24. See R. A. Yoder, *Emerson and the Orphic Poet in America*, 109; and Buell, *New England Literary Culture*, 118.

the ideas are neither imposed nor tacked on. Instead, as we have seen, they grow out of the dilemma of the speaker's experience, a dilemma rooted in Emerson's own experience. "The Problem" *develops* a solution; as R. A. Yoder puts it, "the poem is working out an explanation, not dramatizing one already made."[25] "The Problem" is also pervaded by polarity. Each example in Emerson's long catalogue of expressions of the One (9–62) derives its meaning not only from its being such an expression, but also from its being a denial of monopolistic truth-claims that, given Christian history, are implicit in the poem from the very start. The poet has to assert each non-Christian revelation of truth in the face of its polar opposite, that is, against the view that there is no such thing as non-Christian truth. The poet has to assert, therefore, that the "awful Jove" of Phidias cannot possibly have resulted "from a vain or shallow thought" (9–10), but from a thought as profound as the one inspiring Christianity at its best. Similarly, "the thrilling Delphic oracle" cannot possibly have fallen "from lips of cunning" (11–12). Emerson's examples range far and wide (the pantheistic One, after all, is omnificent), and yet the poem remains coherent because all examples are unified through their denial of the same opposite.

David Porter has said that Emerson's epigrammatic language impoverished his poetry, and often this is the case.[26] In Emerson's best poetry, however, the epigrammatic style condenses, and thus heightens, a richness of reference reminiscent of Goethe's epigrammatic style. This is certainly true of the often epigrammatic couplets in "The Problem." For instance, the idea that great art arises from the depths of spirit could hardly have been expressed more pointedly, and more richly, than by the couplet about the Jove of Phidias. The idea of art's inescapable debt to the organic forms and laws of nature is expressed through an epigrammatic couplet which, in Goethean fashion, lets the thought grow out of and transcend the natural image: "These temples grew as grows the grass; / Art might obey, but not surpass" (45–46). Moreover, note the brilliantly paradoxical couplet: "He builded better than he knew:— / The conscious stone to beauty grew" (23–24). Emerson appreciated the role of the unconscious in artistic creation, as indicated not only by the first line of the couplet just quoted, but also by "The passive Master lent his hand / To the vast soul that o'er him planned" (47–48) and by a journal entry (*JMN* 7:315) dating from the same month in which "The

25. Yoder, *Emerson and the Orphic Poet*, 109.
26. Porter, *Emerson and Literary Change*, 19.

Problem" was completed (November 1839; *PN* 899). The stone, by contrast, becomes "conscious." As long as it was merely part of nature, it remained an unconscious part of the One. Being transformed into a work of art ("to beauty grew"), the stone is imbued with the spirit that works *through* the artist. Art, being "nature passed through the alembic of man" (*CW* 1:17), thus becomes an expression of man's consciousness, even though man himself does not fully grasp—is not fully conscious of— the mysterious power of genius that enables him to create works of art.

In his examination of Goethe's influence on Matthew Arnold's poetry, G. Robert Stange has said that "in Goethe we first find the double notion of seeing the *whole* and seeing things as a whole."[27] As already noted, Goethe adumbrated Hegel's concrete universal. Because Goethe saw "things as a whole," he avoided pursuing a "whole" emptied of reality. The "whole" was for him a concrete presence, a concrete universal, rather than an empty abstraction: "Willst du dich am Ganzen erquicken, / So mußt du das Ganze im Kleinsten erblicken" (If you wish to refresh yourself in the whole, you must perceive the whole in the smallest thing; *GA* 1:410); or "Willst du ins Unendliche schreiten, / Geh nur im Endlichen nach allen Seiten" (If you wish to stride into the infinite, just go into the finite in all directions; *GA* 1:410).

This polarity between the whole as conceptual abstraction and the whole as concrete experience informs such a poem as "The Day's Ration" (*W* 9:138–39). The poem opens with the speaker expressing a sense of limitation, hence of exclusion from the whole:

> When I was born,
> From all the seas of strength Fate filled a chalice,
> Saying, 'This be thy portion, child; this chalice,
> Less than a lily's, thou shalt daily draw
> From my great arteries,—not less, nor more.'
>
> (1–5)

The speaker's first reaction to this fate-imposed limitation is to emphasize the idea suggested by the second line, that his "portion" is a distillation of the whole:

> All substances the cunning chemist Time
> Melts down into the liquor of my life,—
> Friends, foes, joys, fortunes, beauty and disgust.

27. G. Robert Stange, *Matthew Arnold: The Poet as Humanist*, 32.

· ·
All he distils into sidereal wine
And brims my little cup. . . .

(6-8, 11-12)

Such a distillation of the whole is, however, beyond the power of the speaker to grasp. Fate or Time is

        . . . heedless, alas!
Of all he sheds how little it [my little cup] will hold,
How much runs over on the desert sands.
· ·
To-day, when friends approach, and every hour
Brings book, or starbright scroll of genius,
The little cup will hold not a bead more,
And all the costly liquor runs to waste.

(12-14, 20-23)

The speaker now comes to the realization that the whole so conceived is an abstraction posited by the mind as something beyond itself, as something beyond the mind's grasp and thus inaccessible to consciousness. The whole thus becomes a concept emptied of all reality, an unknowable "All" derived dialectically from the mind's sense of its own limitations. The speaker thereupon redefines the whole; it becomes identical with what the mind experiences as a whole, and the smallest thing more than qualifies for wholeness so defined:

Why need I volumes, if one word suffice?
Why need I galleries, when a pupil's draught
After the master's sketch fills and o'erfills
My apprehension? Why seek Italy,
Who cannot circumnavigate the sea
Of thoughts and things at home, but still adjourn
The nearest matters for a thousand days?

(26-32)

"The Day's Ration" succeeds as a poem of ideas. It expresses an intellectual problem arising from the speaker's experience of incompleteness, an experience which is objectified and universalized by the speaker's presenting it as decreed by man's fate. The problem thus rises, as Viëtor has said in connection with Goethe's *Gedankenlyrik*, "to a sphere which lies above the concrete moment and the personal reference."[28] The "I" in the poem becomes a representative "I" mirroring the human condition. Experiencing incompleteness, the speaker feels compelled dialectically to posit a "completeness" and to endeavor to grasp it. Failure to grasp this completeness—a completeness construed as "totality"—leads to the speaker's final insight: the whole is to be found at the opposite extreme from "totality," that is, in the smallest things. In those final lines, the speaker, having abandoned such an abstraction as "totality," becomes specific, direct, and realistic. There is no longer any talk about "sidereal wine" and the "little cup," nor do we find such rhetorical contortions as "Nor gives the jealous lord one diamond drop / So to be husbanded for poorer days" (24–25). Instead we have such simple and direct questions as "Why need I volumes, if one word suffice? / Why need I galleries . . . ? / Why seek Italy . . . ?" In these final lines we also find the "I" reachieving individuality. Finding the whole in small things demands an "I" very different from the generalized "I" that pursued an abstraction; it demands an "I" that is itself a *concrete* universal. In brief compass, the poem thus confronts some very important ideas, and it presents them not statically, but as part of a dialectic involving the self and the reality the self creates or apprehends.

Perhaps the most Goethean of all Emerson's poems of ideas is "The Sphinx." One of Goethe's basic poetic ways of suggesting the mystery at the heart of existence is to present polarities in such a manner as to stress their irreducible tension, their indestructible equilibrium. This approach shapes several poems in the "Gott und Welt" cycle (GA 1:507–33), whose very title, as Gundolf has stressed, does not mean "God and World" as two separate entities, but as a unity—since God contains World and World contains God—that expresses itself in two opposite ways: as God realizing himself in Nature and as Nature embodying God.[29] In Goethe's words, God saw fit "to keep Nature in Himself, and Himself in Nature" (*Natur in Sich, Sich in Natur zu hegen*; GA 1:509). The phrase "Gott und Welt" is therefore as irreducible to distinctness and clarity as the term "Gott-Natur" (GA 1:522) or, for that matter, "Sphinx-Natur" (GA 2:146).

Goethe repeatedly emphasizes the ultimate mystery of nature by means of such polar phrasing. In "Allerdings" we find the well-known lines:

28. Viëtor, *Goethe the Poet*, 231.
29. Gundolf, *Goethe*, 656.

Natur hat weder Kern
Noch Schale,
Alles ist sie mit einem Male.
(*GA* 1:529)

(Nature has neither kernel nor shell; she is everything at once.)

Nature, to put it differently, is an "open secret" (*öffentlich Geheimnis*; *GA* 1:519), itself a polar phrase. The "definition" of nature from "Epirrhema" offers another example of polar phrasing: "Nichts ist drinnen, nichts ist draußen; / Denn was innen, das ist außen" (Nothing is inside and nothing outside since what is within is without; *GA* 1:519). There is also a "definition" of nature in "Parabase":

Klein das Große, groß das Kleine,
. . . .
Immer wechselnd, fest sich haltend,
Nah und fern und fern und nah.
(*GA* 1:516)

(What is big is small, and what is small is big. . . . Always changing, and always invariable. Near and far and far and near.)

In this regard, witness also this statement on the life and vitality of the universe: "Und alles Drängen, alles Ringen / Ist ewige Ruh in Gott dem Herrn" (All this press and struggle is uninterrupted peace in God; *GA* 1:668). It is important to note that in each of these examples Goethe *maintains* the equipollence of both poles. There is no resolution of the tension, no *coincidentia* of opposites, as is so often the case in poetry presenting reality as paradoxical. One might cite Swinburne's "Hertha" or, on a less cosmic level of experience, Baudelaire's "L'Héautontimorouménos" as examples of poems whose polar modes of expression resemble Goethe's but in which a true *coincidentia oppositorum* does occur. For Goethe, existence (*Natur, Gott-Natur, Sphinx-Natur, Gott und Welt*) remains an open question, and his insistently polar phrasing is intended to preclude the possibility of any answer being accepted as finally valid.

"The Sphinx" (*W* 9:20–25) exemplifies Emerson's most successful use of irreducible polarity to state the unanswerable question. Its very title suggests noncoincidence of opposites; the sphinx, after all, is a hybrid. Symbolically, the sphinx may be said to define unanswerability. In Cirlot's words, "Being the supreme embodiment of the enigma, the sphinx keeps watch over an ultimate meaning which must remain for ever beyond the understanding of man."[30] That ungraspable "ultimate meaning" is often held to refer to human nature itself, which so far has defied all attempts at final elucidation. As Madame de Staël put it in a passage Emerson quoted in his journal, "The aenigma of ourselves swallows up like the sphinx thousands of systems which pretend to the glory of having guessed its meaning" (*JMN* 3:51).

In the poem, the Sphinx symbolizes Nature, but a Nature that has risen to consciousness, to self-awareness. The Sphinx, therefore, can no longer simply *be* in the manner of unconscious Nature as represented in stanzas 3–6, where the palm and the elephant and the waves and the atoms and the birds and the babe are said to "enjoy" the natural bliss of unawareness. Having risen to consciousness, the Sphinx, instead of simply *being*, must *know*. Having risen to self-awareness, it cannot escape from the inner compulsion to try to know itself: "Who'll tell me my secret[?]" (5). In the highly dramatic structure of the poem, the Sphinx initially looks for an answer in man, the exemplar *par excellence* of Nature's rise to consciousness. The "Who'll tell me my secret[?]" of the first stanza is, therefore, restated in the second stanza:

> The fate of the man-child,
>   The meaning of man;
> Known fruit of the unknown;
>   Daedalian plan;
> Out of sleeping a waking,
>   Out of waking a sleep;
> Life death overtaking;
>   Deep underneath deep?
>   (9–16)

But man turns out to be a tormented being (49–56). Having attained self-awareness, he can no longer be one of those serene presences in Nature that we find in stanzas 3–6. As we know from the essay on "Experience," "It is very unhappy, but too late to be helped, the discovery we have made, that we exist. That discovery is called the Fall of Man" (*CW* 3:43). Nature herself, as "the great mother," is worried about her human child (57–64).

At this point a poet—who, it should be noted, is distinct from the "I" in the poem—undertakes to solve the riddle of man and hence the riddle

---

30. Juan Eduardo Cirlot, *A Dictionary of Symbols*, 289.

of the Sphinx. In the poet's view, all is for the best in the best of possible worlds:

> Say on, sweet Sphinx! thy dirges
>   Are pleasant songs to me.
> Deep love lies under
>   These pictures of time;
> They fade in the light of
>   Their meaning sublime.
>   (67–72)

> Eterne alternation
>   Now follows, now flies;
> And under pain, pleasure,—
>   Under pleasure, pain lies.
> Love works at the centre,
>   Heart-heaving alway;
> Forth speed the strong pulses
>   To the borders of day.
>   (97–104)

It is this love, according to the poet, that paradoxically causes man's torment. The poet confidently proclaims his understanding of the human condition:

> The fiend that man harries
>   Is love of the Best;
> Yawns the pit of the Dragon,
>   Lit by rays from the Blest.
> The Lethe of Nature
>   Can't trance him again,
> Whose soul sees the perfect,
>   Which his eyes seek in vain.

> To vision profounder,
>   Man's spirit must dive;
> His aye-rolling orb
>   At no goal will arrive;
> The heavens that now draw him
>   With sweetness untold,
> Once found,—for new heavens
>   He spurneth the old.
>   (73–88)

The poet offends the Sphinx both by his arrogance (105–8) and by the patent inadequacy of the solution he has so boldly proclaimed. The solution is inadequate because, like any solution offered by man, it arises from a limited individual perspective and is conditioned by time. Contrary to what the poet says, "these pictures of time" do not "fade in the light of / Their meaning sublime." Instead, they distort that meaning. As Thomas R. Whitaker puts it, the Sphinx, as a "symbol of the Infinite," conveys the idea that should the poet "take his quest through a thousand natures, time would still condition and falsify his reply."[31] Ideally, man may be an "eternity," but actually he is a "clothed eternity," an eternity disfigured by time (119–20). The poet thus fails to solve the riddle of the Sphinx because he cannot solve the riddle of man, who holds the key to the *meaning* of existence.

But this failure has a still deeper significance. It is a failure that consists in the poet's having advanced a solution at all, in his having failed to keep the question "open," in his having provided an "answer" that of necessity violated the infinite "sphinx-ness" of existence. As the Sphinx reminds the poet, this "sphinx-ness" also pervades him: "I am thy spirit, yoke-fellow; / Of thine eye I am eyebeam" (111–12). Indeed, the Sphinx continues,

> Thou art the unanswered question;
>   Couldst see thy proper eye,
> Always it asketh, asketh;
>   And each answer is a lie.
>   (113–16)

If man is the *unanswered* question, the Sphinx's attempt to find an answer to her secret by turning to man (9–16) has failed. Stanza 16, nevertheless, presents the Sphinx as "merry" (121). The stanza celebrates the Sphinx's escape from the prison called "answer" ("Every thought," Emerson said in "The Poet," "is also a prison"; CW 3:19) and her joyful return to a universality forever defying definition:

> Uprose the merry Sphinx,
>   And crouched no more in stone;
> She melted into purple cloud,
>   She silvered in the moon;
> She spired into a yellow flame;
>   She flowered in blossoms red;

31. Thomas R. Whitaker, "The Riddle of Emerson's 'Sphinx,'" 184.

She flowed into a foaming wave:
She stood Monadnoc's head.

Thorough a thousand voices
Spoke the universal dame;
"Who telleth one of my meanings,
Is master of all I am."
(121–32)

Given the Sphinx's reaction to the poet's attempted answer, Whitaker is certainly right in regarding the last two lines as the Sphinx's final taunt. Yoder holds a similar view.[32] The Sphinx's great question, the poem seems to say, is ultimately truer than any answer.

Emerson validates the poem's theme through polarity. Most of the lines I have quoted are part of a larger polar pattern that excludes compromise or any other solution: "Known fruit of the unknown"; "The fiend that man harries / Is love of the Best"; "Yawns the pit of the Dragon, / Lit by rays from the Blest"; "Eterne alternation / Now follows, now flies." Barker Fairley has said that Goethe's notion of polarity closely anticipated the dialectic of a slightly later time.[33] In many of his poems of ideas, however, Goethe, as already indicated, avoids any approximation to a dialectical synthesis: he maintains an absolute polarity as a way of suggesting the insolubleness of the mystery at the center of reality. This is exactly what Emerson does in "The Sphinx." The poem does not evolve toward a reconciliatory transcendence of its antitheses. Man continues to be the *known* fruit of the *unknown*; each answer continues to be a lie; Time remains eternally "the false reply" (120); and the Sphinx is as much a mystery at the conclusion as at the opening. In this sense it may be said that the poem does not develop at all; its meaning lies at the very center of a circle of diametrically opposite assertions. "The Sphinx" is indeed, as David Porter says, "that most inconclusive of all of Emerson's published poems."[34]

32. Whitaker, "The Riddle of Emerson's 'Sphinx,'" 183; Yoder, *Emerson and the Orphic Poet*, 119.
33. Fairley, *Study of Goethe*, 269–70.
34. Porter, *Emerson and Literary Change*, 79–80.

CHAPTER 6

HISTORY AND BIOGRAPHY

Goethe's attitude toward history was nothing if not ambivalent. Though he often expressed indifference or hostility toward history, his negative attitude was mostly limited to certain historiographical claims and methods. He rejected the naive but then common assumption that historians could recapture the past as it had really been. "How little," he told the historian Heinrich Luden, "does even the most extensive work of history contain of the life of a people! And of that little, how little is really true? And of that 'truth,' is anything really beyond doubt?" (GA 22:401). Goethe also perceived the fatal limitation of Enlightenment historiography: he objected to its tendency to measure the achievements of the past entirely by eighteenth-century rationalistic standards. He also responded negatively to certain aspects of the new critical history. Though he commented rather favorably upon Barthold Niebuhr's great *Römische Geschichte* (GA 14:713–14), he deplored the destructive effect of scientific methods like Niebuhr's upon the myth-sustaining capacity of history. Niebuhr's critical study of the sources, though to be applauded from a purely historiographical point of view, had relegated early Roman history, told so inspiringly by Livy, to the "merely fabulous" (GA 24:236). For centuries, Goethe says elsewhere, humanity had derived inspiration from the heroism of a Lucretia or a Mucius Scaevola. "But now historical criticism arrives on the scene and says that those individuals never existed, that instead they should be regarded as fictional, as fabulous creations of the high moral sense of the Romans." However, Goethe concludes in words of the highest importance for our understanding of his philosophy of history, "if the Romans were great enough to invent such heroism, we should at least be great enough to believe in it" (GA 24:162).

Goethe's approach to history, in other words, was mythical, intuitive, and poetic, rather than scientific. In a sense, he regarded scientific exactness in matters historical as a kind of "unbelief," as a failure to respond enthusiastically to the interpretive and creative opportunities afforded man by the lacunae that riddle the record of the human past. His favorite parts of that record were the points at which factual evidence

98

ended and legend (*Sage*) began (*GA* 16:340). Such points provided the most favorable opportunities for creative interpretation. That such interpretation might be misinterpretation did not disturb Goethe: he preferred poetic "superstition" to scientific "unbelief." As he put it in the historical part of the *Farbenlehre*, "superstition is the patrimony of those whose nature is energetic, great-minded, progressive; unbelief belongs to weak, narrow-minded, retrogressive, self-confined men" (*GA* 16:362). In historical thinking, as in history itself, superstition—which is, after all, a form of belief—is fertile and creative, whereas unbelief is sterile (*GA* 3:504–5). Obviously, Goethe was little concerned with historical "truth" as such. Even if it were attainable, what would be the use of the "poor, miserable truth" if it diminished man's spiritual heritage (*GA* 24:162–63)? The only truth that mattered to Goethe was a fruitful, inspiring, life-enhancing truth. Thus, he could say that "the greatest benefit we have received from history is the enthusiasm which it evokes" (*GA* 9:563).

For much of this conception of history Goethe was indebted to his early mentor, Herder. What distinguished him from Herder was his irrepressible artistic tendency to apprehend history through form. In his approach to history, as in his approach to nature or to art, Goethe remained the *Augenmensch*—the man who could apprehend reality only as image, as visual or visualizable form. Whereas Herder dealt with the grand sweep of historical movements, with the great currents of universal history, Goethe selected some objects or persons that he regarded as representing, as symbolizing, the forces and tendencies at work in history. Though the historical part of the *Farbenlehre*, for instance, covers over two thousand years, it does not treat its subject as a history of scientific problems and solutions but illuminates such problems through an examination of the personality traits and historical circumstances of individual scientists. Goethe's portraits of these scientists enable him to "see" the history of science. In Karl Viëtor's words, "The single personality, as it existed in its peculiar force, beauty, and greatness; all its achievements, whether as finished works or as deeds born of the totality of its character; and the ways in which, at the same time, it maintains a living connection with other significant personalities that went before or that were alive and at work at the same time—this is what Goethe likes to contemplate and to depict."[1]

So selective an approach to the past might appear to invalidate any

1. Viëtor, *Goethe the Thinker*, 120.

claim that Goethe was an important historical thinker. What made him such a thinker was precisely his ability to see symbolically the persons, objects, or events he selected. The individual subject acquired for him a concreteness and depth that made it fully itself at the same time it represented many others. His own words on this matter are worth quoting: "Alles was geschieht ist Symbol, und, indem es vollkommen sich selbst darstellt, deutet es auf das übrige" (Everything that happens is symbolic, and in its complete presentation of itself it signifies the rest; GA 21:286). The modernity of such a view is obvious. Goethe's intellectual and aesthetic need "to rise from the individual to the general, and to discover this general primarily in the concrete realization of the individual, became a basic constituent of historicism," Friedrich Meinecke has said. Meinecke's monumental study of the origins of historicism, *Die Entstehung des Historismus*, culminates in a 140-page chapter on Goethe. Wilhelm Emrich has gone so far as to claim that only in our time has historical thinking begun to feel the full impact of Goethe's symbolic approach. Ernst Cassirer also has credited Goethe with having developed new methods in cultural history and in biography, and such a view is fully supported by Friedrich Gundolf.[2]

An appreciation of Emerson's debt to Goethe's symbolic philosophy of history requires a closer look at some of the implications of the latter. Both major emphases in Goethe's conception of symbol play an important role in his historical thinking. First, as we saw in the preceding chapter, the symbol represents, however inadequately, the idea. Second, the symbol is a "particular" representing the "general," that is, a class or group. As representation of the idea, the symbol is truly—to use once more a favorite phrase of Goethe's—an "open secret" (*offenbar Geheimnis*), in that it at one and the same time reveals and hides the idea. Such "hiding" is a necessary condition of revelation: the idea can be revealed only through its achieving embodiment, but such embodiment, as we saw, is of necessity opaque. For the second emphasis—symbol as particular representing the more general ("*wo das Besondere das Allgemeinere repräsentiert*"; GA 9:532)—Goethe often uses the terms *repräsentativ* and *Repräsentant*. In his famous letter to Schiller of 16 August 1797, in which he first clearly stated this second view, he calls symbols "eminent cases [*eminente Fälle*] which . . . as representatives [*Repräsentanten*] of

2. Friedrich Meinecke, *Die Entstehung des Historismus*, 540; Emrich, *Die Symbolik von "Faust II,"* 43; Cassirer, *Goethe und die geschichtliche Welt*, 1–26; Gundolf, *Goethe*, 410–12, 603–38.

many others possess a certain totality . . . and lay claim to a certain oneness and allness [*eine gewisse Einheit und Allheit*]" (*GA* 20:395). Needless to say, both emphases are often present in one and the same symbol.

A few examples. A day spent in wartime Mainz is for Goethe "a symbol of contemporary world history" (*GA* 11:631). Götz von Berlichingen is "the symbol of a significant epoch in world history" (*GA* 10:833). Looking back upon his first twenty-five years from the vantage point of old age, Goethe said he found it worth recalling them because they "contained some symbols of human life" (*GA* 24:493). Of particular interest is the following statement: "The symbolic is often representative [*repräsentativ*]. For instance, the farmer with the dice in *Wallensteins Lager* is a symbolic figure and at the same time a representative one, since he represents his entire class" (*GA* 22:564). The experience at Mainz, Götz, the facts of his youth, the farmer with the dice in Schiller's history play no doubt had their "opaqueness" for Goethe. He remained convinced, nevertheless, that there was no way for man even approximately to grasp the spirit of history *except through such symbols*. Grasping that spirit was not really a matter of acquiring a better understanding of the "laws" of history. It meant, above all, experiencing history in the present, experiencing it aesthetically, so to speak, through creative immersion in its symbols. Two important characteristics of Goethe's historical thinking derive from this symbolic view.

First, there is the strangely atemporal nature of Goethe's sense of history. "Die Gegenwart," he once said, "ist die einzige Göttin, die ich anbete" (The present is the only goddess I adore; *GA* 22:232), and as Cassirer and Meinecke have noted, Goethe had a remarkable ability to see past and present as one.[3] The present is the stage where the experiences that shaped the high moments of history are re-experienced symbolically. As a matter of fact, those "moments" become "high" *only through* our symbolic experience of them. As Emerson explained in an 1835 lecture: "Goethe has remarked that of all history he remembers nothing but a few anecdotes. . . . These incidents, esteemed of trifling importance, when they occurred, are preserved by the moral quality that is in them which makes them always pertinent to human nature whilst laws, expeditions, books, and kingdoms are forgotten" (*EL* 1:250). Goethe was not interested, therefore, in the nostalgic, paralyzing longing

---

3. Cassirer, *Goethe und die geschichtliche Welt*, 11–12; Meinecke, *Die Entstehung des Historismus*, 503–4.

for the past so prevalent in the Germany of his day. True longing, he insisted, was "productive": it stimulated men to re-create, and thus to re-live, what was best in the past (*GA* 23:315; 14:129–30). In the same spirit, Goethe, anticipating Emerson (and Nietzsche), protested against the "burden" of history, against the ever accumulating legacy of the ages that threatens to prevent the present from living a life authentically its own. He spoke of "the dreadful burden . . . that several thousands of years of tradition have rolled upon us," and he congratulated the United States because, unlike Europe, it lived its life untroubled by "useless memories" (*GA* 9:587; 2:405–6). For its virtues as an antidote to the deleterious effects of history, Goethe praised "forgetting," that "precious, heaven-sent gift," which he said he had always known how to "appreciate, use, and augment." As far as history was concerned, Goethe thought it a great advantage "to know little, and of that little to have forgotten much" (*GA* 21:892; 19:670).

Like Goethe, Emerson does not want the present to be paralyzed by "this corpse of . . . memory." Instead, one should "bring the past for judgment into the thousand-eyed present, and live ever in a new day" (*CW* 2:33). Man's chief task, according to Goethe, is not to honor the past but to do his duty. "What is, however, [man's] duty? The demand of the day" (*GA* 9:554). In Emerson's words, "The use of history is to give value to the present hour and its duty" (*W* 7:177). Goethe himself, according to Emerson, had become a historical figure who endowed the present with immense value:

> As history's best use is to enhance our estimate of the present hour so the value of such an observer as Goethe who draws out of our consciousness some familiar fact & makes it glorious by showing it in the light of thought is this: that he makes us prize all our being by suggesting its inexhaustible wealth; for we feel that all our experience is thus convertible into jewels. He moves our wonder at the mystery of our life. (*JMN* 12:189)

What matters concerning history, therefore, is its presentness, not its pastness: "All inquiry into antiquity . . . is the desire to do away this wild, savage and preposterous There or Then, and introduce in its place the Here and the Now" (*CW* 2:7). Put differently: "I feel the eternity of man, the identity of his thought. . . . When a thought of Plato becomes a thought to me . . . time is no more" (*CW* 2:15). The ultimate implications of this debate with history are perhaps summarized most aptly in a passage in *Wilhelm Meisters Lehrjahre* that Emerson copied in his journal in 1832 and seems to have echoed in the opening lines of *Nature* (1836):

I, for my share, cannot understand how men have made themselves believe that God speaks to us thro' books & histories. The man to whom the Universe does not reveal directly what relations it has to him; whose heart does not tell him what he owes himself & others, that man will scarcely learn it out of books which generally do little more than give our errors names. (*JMN* 6:105; *GA* 7:494–95)

In addition to the atemporal nature of Goethe's perception of history, a second characteristic of his historical thinking deserves notice: his intense concentration on the bare facts, the mere events, the insulated individuals, stripped of all the interpretations that have accumulated around them through centuries of historical research and writing. Only that ultimate "source," reduced to its essentials, uncluttered by the viewpoints and analyses of later times, was an expression of the spirit in history and thus had symbolic potential for Goethe. Historical interpretations preceding his own not only distracted from the true instances where spirit had emerged in history, but were, in the nature of things, unacceptable; obviously only Goethe could interpret the symbols of the past in a way satisfactory to Goethe. Emerson fully appreciated this characteristic of Goethe's:

> It is of great entertainment to read Goethe's notices of Kepler, Roger Bacon, Galileo, Newton, Voltaire. Yet they consist of the simplest description almost merely *naming* of the persons from his point of view. . . . Before it is done, one shrinks from such a dark problem as the estimate of a great genius, a Voltaire, a Newton. Yet he has only to address himself to it, to utter the name of the man in a self-contained, self-centred way, & the problem is solved. (*JMN* 7:85)

Emerson's own procedure was similar. He had resolved early (1834), in his "highest most farsighted hours," that his true object in life was "nothing less than to look at every object in its relation to Myself" (*JMN* 4:272), and this resolution also shaped his view of history. Emerson's biographical aperçus and sketches are emphatically Emersonian. What we find is Emerson's Plato, Emerson's Montaigne, Emerson's Shakespeare—figures created out of a bare minimum of facts ("Great geniuses have the shortest biographies"; *CW* 4:25) and given form to symbolize Emerson's intellectual preoccupations as he contemplated the past with the aim of putting it to the service of the present.

Emerson thus shared both Goethe's atemporal sense of history and his symbolically creative approach to a past reduced to some essential facts. Often he also approached history through Goethe's dual conception of symbol: symbol as (inadequate) representation of the idea and symbol as a particular representing the general. The "opaqueness" inherent in the symbol as representation of the idea is evident in passages such as this:

> What is all history but the work of ideas[?] . . . What brought the Pilgrims here? One man says, civil liberty; and another, the desire of founding a church; and a third discovers that the motive force was plantation and trade. But if the Puritans could rise from the dust, they could not answer. It is to be seen in what they were, and not in what they designed. (*CW* 1:134–35)

Emerson then provided his own interpretation of "what they were." Expressing his and his age's imaginative need to see things organically, he regarded the Puritan migration as symbolizing "the growth, the budding and expansion of the human race" (*CW* 1:135). Emerson believed that history is the work of ideas, but, like Goethe, he also recognized that our only way of approximating the ideas is through such opaque, hence multiply interpretable symbols as the Puritan migration. In a similar vein, Emerson claimed that Plato "stands between the truth and every man's mind." Emerson did not mean by this statement, however, that Plato's philosophy merely blocks our direct access to truth. On the contrary, certain aspects of truth are visible *only through* the painted veil of his philosophy. It is simply "impossible to think on certain levels, except through him" (*CW* 4:26). Whatever its limitations, the symbolic approach to history was the only one that Emerson considered to have any validity: "every history should be written in a wisdom which . . . looked at facts as symbols" (*CW* 2:22).

This symbolic view also made it inevitable that Emerson, as the editors of his *Early Lectures* point out, should have inverted "the organic theories of the day to merge history into the individual rather than to merge the individual into the process of history" (*EL* 2:3). The catalyst of this inversion was in all probability Emerson's experience of Italy, during which, as noted earlier, his principal guidebook was Goethe's *Italienische Reise*. Goethe stressed that his encounter with Rome, the city which he considered the pivot of history, had been like a second birth because it had led him to think of history in an entirely new way, as something radiating from a center. "Everywhere else in the world," Goethe wrote, "one observes history from the outside; here one has the feeling that he sees it from within: it is spread all around us and it moves outward from us. And this feeling applies not only to Roman history, but to the history of the whole world" (*GA* 11:160, 167). In Robert D. Richardson's words, Goethe asserts in statements like this "the necessity

of a central experiencing self as the only way to realize . . . history."
Emerson's view became strikingly similar. Italy, Richardson continues,
"gave Emerson his standpoint toward history," a view of history "as all
lying within the experience of each person, and as having meaning solely
as each individual person was able to reexperience it imaginatively."[4]
Having adopted this point of view, Emerson was later able to claim:
"Every history in the world is my history," and "every man, were life long
enough, would write history for himself" (*JMN* 7:389; *CW* 1:107).
Such claims were but other ways of saying that all of history, like all of
nature, is a symbol—however inadequate or opaque—of the soul.

The second Goethean sense of symbol, a particular representing the
general, was perhaps even more important to Emerson's historical thinking. As indicated above, Goethe often substituted "representative" (*Repräsentant, repräsentativ*) for symbol (*Symbol*) in this sense. A few examples:

> Every moment is of infinite worth because it is the *Repräsentant* of the whole
> of eternity. (*GA* 24:67)

> This eminent man [Wieland] may be regarded as the *Repräsentant* of his age.
> (*GA* 3:555)

> Privy Councillor Blumenbach . . . [was] a true *Repräsentant* of the great
> institution of learning in which he had worked for so many years as its most
> distinguished member. (*GA* 11:931)

> It was precisely in his hatred of Napoleon and of the French that Walter Scott
> was the true interpreter and *Repräsentant* of English popular opinion and of
> English patriotic feeling. (*GA* 24:708)

> [Plato and Aristotle] as separate *Repräsentanten* of splendid, not easy to
> combine qualities divide, so to speak, mankind between them. (*GA* 16:347)

> [Thylesius] appears to us as the *Repräsentant* of many of his contemporaries
> who treated scientific matters elegantly while feeling it necessary to support
> elegance with scholarship. (*GA* 16:383)

This concept of representativeness is, to be sure, much older than
Goethe's expression of it. Edmund G. Berry has traced it to ancient
Stoicism and Plutarch.[5] The person chiefly responsible for its vogue in
modern times, however, seems to have been Herder. According to Herder, "The individual . . . is inescapably a member of some group; conse-

---

4. Robert D. Richardson, Jr., "Emerson's Italian Journey," 124, 126.
5. Berry, *Emerson's Plutarch*, 92–93.

quently all that he does must express, consciously or unconsciously, the aspirations of his group." The most eloquent such expresser is the artist. Herder stressed repeatedly that "the true artist (in the widest sense) creates only out of the fullness of the experience of his whole society. . . . The artist is a sacred vessel which is shaped by, and the highest expression of, the spirit of his time and place and society." This concentration on the artist does not seriously limit the applicability of Herder's concept of representativeness since he insisted throughout his life that "all men are in some degree artists."[6] Herder's immense influence made his ideas the common property of thinkers in late eighteenth-century Germany, whence they spread throughout Europe. An English translation of his *Ideen zur Philosophie der Geschichte der Menschheit* (1784–1791) appeared in London in 1800 (*L* 1:153 n. 62). As early as 1808, Herder's ideas were discussed in *The Monthly Anthology*, a Boston review of which Emerson's father, the Reverend William Emerson, had been an early editor.[7] At any rate, by the 1820s New England intellectuals could hardly have been unfamiliar with the Herderian idea of representativeness. Edward Everett expressed it thus in his Phi Beta Kappa oration at Harvard in 1824:

> Literature . . . is the voice of the age and the state. The character, energy, and resources of the country, are reflected and imaged forth in the conceptions of its great minds. They are the organs of the time; they speak not their own language, they scarce think their own thoughts; but under an impulse like the prophetic enthusiasm of old, they must feel and utter the sentiments which society inspires. They do not create, they obey the Spirit of the Age.[8]

Emerson, a youthful individualist at the time, found the idea disturbing. As he wrote to his aunt Mary Moody Emerson: "I have not forgiven Everett one speculative doctrine of the Φ B K oration, the more disagreeable, that I have found some reason to think it true,—to wit, that geniuses are the organs, mouthpieces of their age; do not speak their own words, nor think their own thoughts" (*J* 2:100–101). He also showed his awareness of the doctrine's ancient roots: "'T is not in man to thank the philosopher that merges his selfish in the social nature. 'T was a foolish vanity in the Stoic to talk in this wise" (*J* 2:101).

Scholars have traced Emerson's doctrine of representativeness to

6. Isaiah Berlin, *Vico and Herder: Two Studies in the History of Ideas*, 201, 203–4.

7. Pochmann, *German Culture in America*, 110; Frank Luther Mott, *A History of American Magazines*, 1:253–54; Rusk, *Life of Ralph Waldo Emerson*, 18, 27.

8. Edward Everett, *Orations and Speeches, on Various Occasions*, 25.

sources more modern and more specifically relevant than the Stoics, among them Swedenborg, Cousin, and the American Puritan tradition.[9] Each of these may have contributed to Emerson's understanding and acceptance of the concept, as undoubtedly did Everett and also the ideals of American democracy.[10] But of all possible sources Goethe proved most fruitful to Emerson. I am not just referring to Goethe's frequent and emphatic use of the term "representative," nor to the term's symbolic depth in his use of it. Even more important are the biographical sketches Goethe wrote—sketches which, informed by the concept of representativeness and exemplifying new biographical methods, could serve as models for *Representative Men*.

Of course, Emerson was exposed to Goethe's speculations on representativeness long before he delivered his lectures in *Representative Men* (1845–1846; published 1850). He showed great interest in Goethe's discussion of the archetypal plant (*Urpflanze*) in the *Italienische Reise* (*JMN* 4:282, 289; 5:138). By *Urpflanze* Goethe did not mean a primordial plant from which all other plants had developed in the course of evolution; rather, he thought of it as the essential plant archetypally present in all existing plants (*GA* 11:291, 353). As such it was "eine symbolische Pflanze," (a symbolical plant; *GA* 16:867). The *Urpflanze* was indeed one of those archetypal phenomena (*Urphänomene*) which Goethe considered symbolical in the sense of representative. The *Urphänomen* is "symbolical because it comprises all cases" (*symbolisch, weil es alle Fälle begreift*; *GA* 9:672). Of similar symbolic import was Goethe's final experience of a massive monumentality like the Colosseum's, which became for him "an incalculable summation" (*ein unübersehbares summa summarum*) of all his Roman experiences (*GA* 11:611). Moreover, whereas "Swedenborg & Behmen saw that things were representative [but] did not sufficiently see that men were" (*JMN* 9:342), Goethe did not fail to convey in the *Italienische Reise* his sense that men were as representative as things. For instance, he characterizes a travelling companion, a captain in the papal army, as "a true representative [*ein wahrer Repräsentant*] of many of his countrymen" (*GA* 11:124).

9. For Swedenborg, see Paul Sakmann, *Ralph Waldo Emerson's Geisteswelt*, 133; and Matthiessen, *American Renaissance*, 632. For Cousin, see Kenneth Kurtz, "The Sources and Development of Emerson's *Representative Men*," 76; John O. McCormick, "Emerson's Theory of Human Greatness," 303–4, 311; and Van Cromphout, "Emerson and the Dialectics of History," 58. For the Puritan heritage, see Sacvan Bercovitch, *The Puritan Origins of the American Self*, 174–78.

10. Perry Miller, "Emersonian Genius and the American Democracy."

Given Goethe's sense, frequently expressed in the *Italienische Reise* and throughout his works, of the representativeness of persons as well as of things, and given Emerson's familiarity with Goethe's works, it seems likely that Goethe was the major factor in Emerson's tendency, noticeable as early as the mid-1830s, to think of historical figures as representative. "Homer," we read in an 1835 journal, "is to us nothing personal, merely the representative of his time. I believe that to be his sincerest use & worth" (*JMN* 5:50). In the lectures in *Biography* (1835), Luther's representativeness resides in his illustrating the "truth, that those talents and means which operate great results on society, are those which are common to all men" (*EL* 1:119). Somewhat less universally, Luther, according to an 1835 notebook, is "a representative" of "objective religion," and this makes him also, of course, a representative of all those practicing "objective religion" (*JMN* 12:41). In the lectures in *English Literature* (1835–1836), Emerson calls Chaucer "the representative of the entire humanity of that period" (*EL* 1:272). Indeed, "Genius is always representative", and hence "all worthy men feel a warm brotherhood to the seers" (*EL* 3:81–82). "Every thinker," we are told elsewhere, "is representative" (*JMN* 8:67). The power of the great orator resides in his representativeness, in his "simply saying what we would but cannot say" (*EL* 3:82). On the same grounds, "the poet is representative" (*CW* 3:4, 5). Alfieri, for instance, is a poet whose "rare opportunities & the determination to use them, make him a valuable representative" (*JMN* 9:465). All history, in sum, is but "the group of the types or representative men of any age" (*JMN* 10:289).

Though many of Goethe's and Emerson's representative men were undoubtedly "great," both writers appear—unlike, say, Plutarch or Carlyle—"anti-heroic" in that they stress the *representativeness* rather than the greatness or uniqueness of their subjects. As just one example from Goethe, let us take the opening sentences of his biographical sketch of Benvenuto Cellini:

> In so active a city [Florence], in so important an age [early sixteenth century], there appeared a man who may be considered the *Repräsentant* of his century and perhaps the *Repräsentant* of all mankind. Individuals like him can be regarded as spiritual fuglemen [*Flügelmänner*], who exhibit through vigorous expression that which is fully inscribed, though often only in faint and unreadable characters, in every human heart.
>
> More specifically, however, he appears, by the range of his talents, as the *Repräsentant* of the artistic class [*Künstlerklasse*]. (*GA* 15:894)

Goethe could hardly have been more emphatic about Cellini's representativeness: the thrice-repeated *Repräsentant*, the striking *Flügelmänner*, the embedding of Cellini in a specific time and place, the varying scope of his representativeness (the sixteenth century, all mankind, the artists), Cellini's not being mentioned by name (Goethe does not do so until the sixth paragraph)—all alert us to the fact that Goethe will deemphasize Cellini's uniqueness, his independence from circumstances, his originality. Such an approach is all the more remarkable in view of Cellini's well-known personality traits: he was exceptional, eccentric, and vagabondish.

Emerson's approach in *Representative Men* is exactly the same: "*Great men*: the word is injurious. . . . All men are at last of a size" (*CW* 4:17–18). Napoleon, whom most nineteenth-century writers regarded as a Titan at war with himself, a Promethean benefactor of mankind, or an Attila-like *flagellum Dei*—in any case, a *heroic* figure—appears to Emerson as a bourgeois who "owes his predominance to the fidelity with which he expresses the tone of thought and belief, the aims of the masses of active and cultivated men" of the nineteenth century (*CW* 4:129). Similarly, Emerson holds that Plato "is a great average man . . . so that men see in him their own dreams and glimpses made available, and made to pass for what they are" (*CW* 4:34). Like all of Emerson's representative men, Plato "consumed his own times" (*CW* 4:24). In fact, "the greatest genius is the most indebted man" (*CW* 4:109). Shakespeare, for instance, was "more distinguished by range and extent, than by originality" (*CW* 4:109). The representative man, in short, "finds himself in the river of the thoughts and events, forced onward by the ideas and necessities of his contemporaries. He stands where all the eyes of men look one way, and their hands all point in the direction in which he should go" (*CW* 4:109).[11]

As author of *Representative Men*, Emerson also benefitted from Goethe's experiments as a biographer. It was Emerson's adoption of Goethe's biographical method that made *Representative Men* so different from the lectures in *Biography* (1835), where Emerson's method, as Edmund G. Berry has shown, was Plutarchan. Plutarch was the most prominent ancient practitioner of the "moral biography," a genre with methodological requirements of its own. In a Plutarchan biography, Berry points out, we find "the biographical facts briefly stated, with the chief emphasis laid on the character of the individual, which will be

---

11. On representativeness as distinguished from greatness, see Joel Porte, *Representative Man: Ralph Waldo Emerson in His Time*, 318–20; and Mark Patterson, "Emerson, Napoleon, and the Concept of the Representative," 233–34.

illumined by quotation and anecdote. . . . The characters portrayed will tend to be treated as heroes and given heroic stature." Berry convincingly demonstrates that *Biography* and some of Emerson's other biographical sketches largely exemplify this method.[12] Berry makes no claim, however, about *Representative Men* being in any way Plutarchan in method.

Scholars have repeatedly stressed the novelty of Goethe's biographical method.[13] Goethe was apparently the first to break definitively with the traditional ethical/characterological emphasis in biography. Instead, he exemplified the then revolutionary approach of treating his biographical subjects as inextricably involved in the conditions of their time and country, and in questions and issues transcending their time and country. His protagonists are thus inseparable from a certain historical environment, with which they interact to define themselves and develop, but at the same time their aspirations and endeavors enable Goethe to turn them into vehicles for the exploration of problems and questions whose significance transcends that historical environment. Goethe's *Repräsentanten*, in other words, are representative not only of a historically circumscribed context, but also of thoughts and preoccupations relevant to humanity as a whole. We saw this dual representation indicated at the beginning of the biographical sketch of Cellini. Another example is provided by *Winckelmann und sein Jahrhundert* (*Winckelmann and His Century*), whose very title already suggests a concern with historical representativeness, which is indeed an important emphasis in the work. But Goethe's examination of Winckelmann's career also leads him to reflections on such matters as the pagan mentality, the differences between ancient and modern friendship, the nature of beauty, the rise and fall of the arts, bibliophilism, patronage, religious conversion, and the pretensions of philosophers—subjects having implications and relevance transcending Winckelmann's immediate historical situation. It is also worth pointing out that Goethe's sense of form does not desert him in a work like *Winckelmann*: the protagonist is integrally related to his age, and the more "universal" reflections arise naturally from Winckelmann's career as Goethe sketches it.

12. Berry, *Emerson's Plutarch*, 20, 258–68.

13. See Reinhard Schuler, *Das Exemplarische bei Goethe: Die biographische Skizze zwischen 1803 und 1809*; Ursula Wertheim, "Zu Problemen von Biographie und Autobiographie in Goethes Ästhetik"; Hans Meyer, "Der Weg zur Geschichte: *Dichtung und Wahrheit*"; Karl Joachim Weintraub, *The Value of the Individual: Self and Circumstance in Autobiography*, 336–76; Gundolf, *Goethe*, 603–38; and Albrecht Dihle, *Studien zur griechischen Biographie*, 87.

Emerson's method in *Representative Men* is identical to Goethe's. His chapters show the same interweaving of the individual with his historical background and with ideas having relevance far beyond that background. In this regard, Emerson's observations concerning Swedenborg's historical representativeness are especially telling:

> Swedenborg was born into an atmosphere of great ideas. 'Tis hard to say what was his own. . . . Harvey had shown the circulation of the blood: Gilbert had shown that the earth was a magnet: Descartes, taught by Gilbert's magnet with its vortex, spiral, and polarity, had filled Europe with the leading thought of vortical motion, as the secret of nature. Newton, in the year in which Swedenborg was born, published the "Principia," and established the Universal Gravity. Malpighi, following the high doctrines of Hippocrates, Leucippus, and Lucretius, had given emphasis to the dogma, that Nature works in leasts, "tota in minimis existit natura." Unrivalled dissectors, Swammerdam, Leeuwenhoek, Winslow, Eustachius, Heister, Vesalius, Boerhaave, had left little for scalpel or microscope to reveal in human or comparative anatomy: Linnaeus, his contemporary, was affirming in his beautiful science, that "Nature is always like herself:" and, lastly, the nobility of method, the largest application of principles had been exhibited by Leibnitz and Christian Wolff, in Cosmology; whilst Locke and Grotius had drawn the moral argument. What was left for a genius of the largest calibre, but to go over their ground, and verify and unite? It is easy to see in these minds the origin of Swedenborg's studies, and the suggestion of his problems. He had a capacity to entertain and vivify these volumes of thought. Yet the proximity of these geniuses, one or other of whom had introduced all his leading ideas, makes Swedenborg another example of the difficulty, even in a highly fertile genius, of proving originality, the first birth and annunciation of one of the laws of nature. (*CW* 4:59–60)

But Swedenborg's endeavors also led Emerson to reflect upon such epoch-transcending topics as the superiority of the contemplative class (poets, philosophers, moralists), the primacy of the moral sentiment, the deadening effect of traditional theology, the nature of symbolism, the meaning of love, and nature's continuous metamorphosis.

When Goethe wanted to establish the cultural atmosphere in which Cellini developed, he simply listed thirty-two artists contemporary with Cellini and told the reader to recall their achievements. Such a long list emphasizes once again Cellini's representativeness: he is a great artist among thirty-two other great artists. Emerson's Shakespeare is representative of a similar constellation of genius: "Kyd, Marlow, Greene, Jonson, Chapman, Dekker, Webster, Heywood, Middleton, Peele, Ford, Massinger, Beaumont, and Fletcher" (*CW* 4:111). This list, while firmly establishing Shakespeare in his historical context, also reinforces a more general theme preoccupying Emerson in this biographical sketch: the connections among genius, originality, and indebtedness. Shakespeare's career, moreover, leads Emerson to discuss the ever-relevant question of the failure of genius to be recognized by contemporaries. Further reflections address such matters as the inadequacies of biography and the failings of poetry not rooted in experience. As in Goethe's biographical sketches, the three concerns—Shakespeare, his historical milieu, and the larger questions suggested by his achievement—skillfully interweave.

Sometimes Goethe begins a biographical sketch with general reflections on a universally relevant subject and then concretizes the subject by making the protagonist its representative embodiment. An example is his treatment of Roger Bacon in the historical part of the *Farbenlehre*. Leading up to Bacon is a long introduction on the nature of authority and the ways in which men in general and scientists in particular respond to authority and, more specifically, to the authority inherent in tradition. The best minds, Goethe concludes, master the traditional learning and accept its authority; at the same time, they maintain their independence and show their originality by renewing and transforming the tradition. A man representing this combination of tradition and originality was Roger Bacon, whom Goethe then presents in his historical context. Bacon's efforts within that context, in their turn, lead Goethe to additional reflections on such "universal" subjects as mathematics, superstition, and unbelief (*GA* 16:349–62). The long introduction establishes the angle of vision from which the protagonist and his historical context are primarily viewed. Though the reflective, biographical, and historical parts complement each other, the extensive and arresting introductory reflections set the tone for and define the scope of the ensuing discussion.

In *Representative Men* this approach is most evident in "Montaigne," where seven of the chapter's twenty pages are taken up by a splendid introduction in which Montaigne is not even mentioned. Emerson discusses at length materialism and idealism, two interpretations of reality that are both "wrong by being in extremes." A third way of looking at reality is skepticism, which occupies "the middle ground between these two" (*CW* 4:88). After extensive comment on skepticism and the qualities of the skeptic, Emerson finally finds concrete focus: "These qualities meet in the character of Montaigne" (*CW* 4:92). He then devotes some pages to Montaigne's personal history, character, and writings, all of which illustrate skepticism as defined in the introductory section, as when he says that Montaigne's writing "has no enthusiasms, no aspiration; contented, selfrespecting, and keeping the middle of the road" (*CW* 4:95–96). Montaigne's fundamental wisdom consisted, however, in his "knowing that we cannot know" (*CW* 4:98); his personal motto, after all, was *Que sçais-je?* Therefore, Montaigne had no illusions about skepticism's being in any way the "final" answer. His skepticism about skepticism leads to a concluding section of almost nine pages long, in which Emerson returns to general theoretical questions about skepticism and denies it the "centrality" that he ascribed to it in the opening section:

> The final solution in which Skepticism is lost, is, in the moral sentiment, which never forfeits its supremacy. . . . I play with the miscellany of facts and take those superficial views which we call Skepticism but I know that they will presently appear to me in that order which makes Skepticism impossible. A man of thought must feel the thought that is parent of the universe: that the masses of nature do undulate and flow. (*CW* 4:103)

Although Emerson's piece on Montaigne confronts general questions more extensively than do the other biographies in *Representative Men*, such questions play a prominent part in all of them, as is suggested by their very titles: "Plato, or the Philosopher," "Swedenborg, or the Mystic," "Shakespeare, or the Poet," and so on. Mostly, of course, the general reflections are more closely interwoven with the biographical and historical parts than they are in "Montaigne, or the Skeptic." "Goethe, or the Writer," however, does resemble "Montaigne" (and Goethe's account of Roger Bacon) by starting with a five-page introduction that does not mention Goethe by name but sets the stage for his appearance. Emerson discusses the "writer," who is "an organic agent in nature" (*CW* 4:153). As such, he is as indispensable to the world as any other "organic agent": "I find a provision in the constitution of the world for the writer or secretary, who is to report the doings of the miraculous spirit of life that everywhere throbs and works" (*CW* 4:151). After extensive examination of the writer's characteristics, obligations, and privileges, Emerson turns to the nineteenth century and to the special problems and questions then confronting the "spirit of life" in its need to be "reported." "Some reply to these questions," Emerson suggests, "may be furnished by looking over the list of men of literary genius in our age. Among these, no more instructive name occurs than that of Goethe, to represent the powers and duties of the scholar or writer" (*CW* 4:155–56). The remaining eleven pages of "Goethe, or the Writer" are devoted to Goethe as representative of the *mind* of the nineteenth century (as distinguished from Napoleon, the "representative of the popular external life and aims of the nineteenth century"; CW 4:156).

These examples will suffice to show how utterly different *Representative Men* is from the lectures in *Biography*. The earlier work was largely Plutarchan in its intense concentration on the protagonist; in its moral, characterological, heroic emphases; in its presenting actions and behavior anecdotally and making them serve the demands of characterization, something which has structural as well as thematic implications. *Representative Men*, on the other hand, is Goethean, first of all in its insistence that the protagonist is inseparable from his historical context. What Emerson says about Goethe is equally applicable to all his representative men: Goethe would have been "impossible at any earlier time" (CW 4:156). The more a Shakespeare, a Swedenborg, a Goethe absorbs and molds the culture of his age, the greater a figure he is. After all, "What is a great man, but one of great affinities, who takes up into himself all arts, sciences, all knowables, as his food? he can spare nothing; he can dispose of every thing" (CW 4:24). According to Albrecht Dihle, such a historical approach would have been unavailable to Plutarch both because the ancients had no sense of historical periods as essentially different from each other and because in antiquity biographical interest was directed toward the ethical rather than the historical.[14] *Representative Men* is Goethean also in its speculative orientation: the lives of the protagonists point to questions and problems of universal human significance. Finally, *Representative Men* is Goethean in the ways in which it structures and organizes its biographical, historical, and speculative interests.

Emerson certainly was a great admirer of Plutarch, but in the decade following the lectures in *Biography*, he came to realize that if he wanted to be a modern biographer, he could not remain a Plutarchan biographer. The nineteenth century, after all, was "the Reflective or Philosophical age" (CW 1:66). It was also an age, as Hegel pointed out, when an increasing awareness of the highly developed and complex state of civilization made truly independent achievement next to impossible.[15] If Emerson wanted to be a modern biographer, he had to treat his subjects as historically and philosophically representative. The man who showed him the way, in this as in so much else, was Goethe. Goethe not only embodied representativeness, in the dual sense of the term, but he also

14. Dihle, *Studien zur griechischen Biographie*, 87.
15. Hegel, *Vorlesungen über die Aesthetik*, in *Sämtliche Werke*, 12:245–68.

wrote biographies informed by the dual concept of representativeness. It is altogether fitting that *Representative Men* should have for its finale a chapter on Goethe, *the* representative writer of the nineteenth century, part of whose representativeness consisted in his having written biographies appropriate to the age, that is to say, biographies treating their subjects as representative.

CHAPTER 7

THE MODERN INDIVIDUAL

As we saw in chapter 1, Goethe appeared to the nineteenth century as the writer who had rendered most poignantly and most authoritatively the problems and pains of the radically divided self. Goethe was not satisfied, however, with merely diagnosing the sickness of the self: he engaged in a reinterpretation of the self designed to overcome its contradictions and antinomies and to reachieve a sense of coherence and integrity. What Goethe attempted was no less than a reconstruction of the self. He accomplished this reconstruction by reintegrating the self and "the other," and he achieved such reintegration by endowing the self with an autonomy and individualism that were, if anything, more radical, more fundamental, than the autonomy and individualism claimed for it by most of his contemporaries.

There is widespread agreement among scholars that individualism as we know it arose in the age of Goethe. Karl Joachim Weintraub, for instance, advances the thesis that "individuality is a specifically modern form of self-conception" some of whose features are traceable to the Renaissance but whose full development had to await "the time of Goethe." Quite appropriately, Weintraub ends *The Value of the Individual*, his learned historical survey of "Self and Circumstance in Autobiography," with a chapter on Goethe's *Dichtung und Wahrheit*. Lionel Trilling also regards the age of Goethe as seminal in this respect: "The self that makes itself manifest at the end of the eighteenth century is different in kind, and in effect, from any self that had ever before emerged." Fritz Martini points specifically to Goethe as the culmination of the individualistic tendencies that affected so powerfully the Romantic movement. Goethe's personality and work were the supreme expressions of an era whose hallmark was "individual consciousness experiencing itself in all its depth, developing itself forcefully, and suffering profound disturbance." It was the era of "individualism demanding autonomy" and having to bear the burden of its freedom. Concentrating on *Faust* as representing the essence of Goethe's legacy, Marshall Berman has said that it opened up "new dimensions in the emerging modern self-awareness." According to Jacques Barzun, "Faust's life is the life of every man," but it owes this representativeness to the basic message of *Faust*, which is that the lesson Faust learns has to be "relearned individually through experience." This emphasis on *individual experience* also made *Faust* "the gospel of the romantic life."[1]

Goethe may be said to have "secularized" the idea of individuality. He saw the individual life as deriving its value or significance not from its role or place in an overarching religious or metaphysical system, but from its being *life* and *individual*, from the very fact that it existed and was unique. Individuality thus became valuable in and of itself. Goethe insisted, furthermore, that each individual life was incommensurable, and that it consisted in unending creation and transformation. But while stressing the uniqueness of each individual, he also knew that "the never-resting process of individuation inevitably meant a ceaseless interaction of a growing self with an ever-different world configuration. . . . A self could not value itself apart from its world."[2]

Emerson had some reservations about Goethe's theory and practice of individualism, but in general his response was far less critical than some of his remarks in *Representative Men* might lead one to suppose. In this work he accused Goethe, among other things, of making truth subservient to self-culture:

> His is not even the devotion to pure truth; but to truth for the sake of culture. He has no aims less large than the conquest of universal nature, of universal truth to be his portion. . . . [He has] one test for all men, *What can you teach me?* All possessions are valued by him for that only; rank, privileges, health, time, being itself. (*CW* 4:163)

As a result of such all-consuming concern with his own development, Goethe "can never be dear to men" (*CW* 4:163). But in his journals and elsewhere, Emerson repeatedly undercuts this well-known criticism. "I claim for him," Emerson wrote in August 1836, "the praise of truth, of fidelity to his nature" (*JMN* 5:133). This equation of "fidelity to his nature" with "truth" is something one might expect from the Emerson who wrote in his most famous essay: "Nothing is at last sacred but the integrity of your own mind" (*CW* 2:30). Similarly, in his essay on

---

1. Weintraub, *Value of the Individual*, xiv; Lionel Trilling, *The Opposing Self*, ix; Fritz Martini, *Deutsche Literaturgeschichte: Von den Anfängen bis zur Gegenwart*, 111; Marshall Berman, *All That Is Solid Melts into Air: The Experience of Modernity*, 39; Jacques Barzun, *Classic, Romantic and Modern*, 87.
2. Weintraub, *Value of the Individual*, 336.

"Character," Emerson, far from blaming Goethe's concern with self-culture, actually praises it:

> Those who live to the future must always appear selfish to those who live to the present. Therefore it was droll in the good Riemer, who has written memoirs of Goethe, to make out a list of his donations and good deeds. . . . A man is a poor creature, if he is to be measured so. . . . The true charity of Goethe is to be inferred from the account he gave Dr. Eckermann, of the way in which he had spent his fortune. "Each bon-mot of mine has cost a purse of gold. Half a million of my own money, the fortune I inherited, my salary, and the large income derived from my writings for fifty years back, have been expended to instruct me in what I now know." (*CW* 3:60–61)

Goethe's example was also decisive in inducing Emerson to prefer the German idea of culture to the English:

> Culture—how much meaning the Germans affix to the word & how unlike to the English sense. The Englishman goes to see a museum or a mountain for itself; the German for himself; the Englishman for entertainment, the German for culture. The German is conscious, & his aims are great. The Englishman lives from his eyes, & immersed in the apparent world. (*JMN* 5:303)

In view of his occasional complaints about Goethe's "lowness" and vulgarity, it is interesting to note that Emerson adds: "Our culture comes not alone from the grand & beautiful, but also from the trivial & sordid" (*JMN* 5:303). The Goethean influence is also discernible in the lectures on *Human Culture*, as when Emerson says that "Culture aim[s] ever at the perfection of the Man himself as the end" or "It may be stated as the end of Culture to teach us to Be" (*EL* 2:312, 298).

"Culture," however, presupposes something to be cultivated. According to Goethe, nature has endowed each human being with an inescapable and indestructible core of identity, which he variously calls "Dämon," "Charakter," or "Monade." The "Dämon," we learn from the philosophical poem "Urworte: Orphisch" (*GA* 1:523–24), is a "Geprägte Form," a form minted and impressed by nature that neither time nor influence can negate. Commenting upon "Urworte: Orphisch," Goethe explained that the daimon is the immutable, ineluctable, and limiting core of identity given every individual at birth (*GA* 2:617). In a manuscript of "Urworte: Orphisch," Goethe translated the Greek term "Daimon" into "Charakter."[3] He was justified in doing so because etymologically "character"

3. Erich Trunz, ed., *Goethe-Gedichte*, 674.

is another "Geprägte Form," since the Greek original of "character" means "stamp," "mark," and hence "distinctive nature." It is of the utmost importance, Karl Viëtor has said, that we understand that for Goethe character is a force of nature, that it is the controlling principle, the inviolable law of an individual's nature.[4] Goethe's third term, "Monade," has, of course, Leibnizian connotations, something Goethe was well aware of (*GA* 24:399). "Monade" in its turn emphasizes that the core of individuality is indestructible (*unverwüstlich*; *GA* 22:675), irreducible (a result of its *Hartnäckigkeit*, its innate tenacity; *GA* 24:399), and undeflectable (Nature's highest gift to man is "die rotierende Bewegung des Monas um sich selbst" [the rotating movement of the monad around itself; *GA* 9:543]).

Emerson was aware of the synonymity of Goethe's terms, as is apparent from an 1837 journal entry: "Character is what the German means when he speaks of the Daimonisches. A strong monad is strong to live as well as to think, & this is the last resource" (*JMN* 5:318). Though he does not yet distinguish between the Goethean concepts of *Dämonisches* and *Dämon*, he obviously means the latter; two years later he shows his awareness of the meaning of the former concept when, in his lecture on "Demonology," he quotes and discusses Goethe's famous statement on *das Dämonische* in book 20 of *Dichtung und Wahrheit* (*EL* 3:163–64). The second sentence of the journal passage just quoted echoes Goethe's repeated insistence that while every monad is indestructible, some are stronger than others and consequently assert themselves more forcefully (e.g., *GA* 22:674–76). Such assertiveness may be called "egotism," a generally negative concept which both Goethe and Emerson rehabilitated because they considered it a prerequisite for self-culture. Only the purest and most vigorous egotism (*Egoismus*), Goethe says, will allow the individual to prevail (*GA* 14:915). For Emerson, egotism "has its root in the cardinal necessity by which each individual persists to be what he is. This individuality is not only not inconsistent with culture, but is the basis of it" (*W* 6:134). Moreover, the greater an individual's accomplishments, the more significant the contributions of egotism: "Take egotism out, and you would castrate the benefactors. Luther, Mirabeau, Napoleon, John Adams, Andrew Jackson . . . would lose their vigor" (*JMN* 15:349–50).

Emerson recognized as fully as Goethe the inescapable limitations that individuality imposes upon the self. He found his self-assertive essay

4. Karl Viëtor, *Goethes Anschauung vom Menschen*, 40.

on "Self-Reliance" as good a place as any to remind his audience of those limitations: "I suppose no man can violate his nature. All the sallies of his will are rounded in by the law of his being as the inequalities of Andes and Himmaleh are insignificant in the curve of the sphere" (CW 2:34). But neither Goethe nor Emerson accepted determinism. Arnold Bergstraesser neatly summarizes Goethe's view on the matter: "As a creature, man is subject to his nature. As a free creature, he is able to search for the universal intention inherent in his nature, to formulate it, and to shape himself."[5] Emerson's position is equally subtle: "Man is made of the same atoms as the world is, he shares the same impressions, predispositions and destiny. When his mind is illuminated, when his heart is kind, he throws himself joyfully into the sublime order, and does, with knowledge, what the stones do by structure" (W 6:240). The key phrase here is "with knowledge." Knowledge allows man the freedom of speculation, of interpretation, of giving meaning and value; through consciousness and perception he shapes both himself and the world in which he lives. We can approach this matter from a somewhat different angle if we remember that Goethe's idea of *Steigerung* (enhancement) finds its ultimate expression in the human individual because in him nature rises to consciousness, to self-awareness. Or in Emerson's words, "What is a man but nature's finer success in self-explication?" (CW 2:209). Needless to say, this success is far from complete. To the end of his days, Goethe accepted as valid the thought he had shared with Lavater in 1780: "Individuum est ineffabile" (GA 18:533). In Emerson's version, "Hard as it is to describe God, it is harder to describe the Individual" (JMN 5:337). At the very moment in cultural history that individuality became the central and inescapable reality, it also became a mystery to itself. Man is nature in the *process* of achieving self-awareness, and no one knows what nature's next step toward self-knowledge will reveal. But it is this very indeterminacy that gives man scope and freedom and shaping power.

In this context the fourth term that Goethe used to designate what is irreducibly individual in man, "Entelechie," becomes relevant because it introduces the idea of development. "Entelechie" is "Dämon" or "Charakter" or "Monade" in the process of self-development and self-realization. The essence of man is not just "Geprägte Form" (a form minted and impressed by nature), but "Geprägte Form, die lebend sich entwickelt" (a minted form engaged in vital self-development; GA 1:524). Goethean,

5. Arnold Bergstraesser, *Goethe's Image of Man and Society*, 158.

or for that matter Emersonian, individuality is not something complete at its inception, but something man has to explore, pursue, create. Goethe, as Ortega y Gasset put it, "traversed his life in search of Goethe, in search of that figure of himself which he felt called upon to realize, to bring into the real."[6] Individuality, in other words, is the self in search of self-realization.

But how can a "Geprägte Form" be subject to change and development? To put it differently, how can something as immutable and as tenaciously itself as the *Dämon* or the *Monade* change at all? Goethe's answer was that it could change and yet remain itself because the change was a matter of metamorphosis. It is, after all, of the essence of metamorphosis that earlier forms are not obliterated but *aufgehoben*, in the Hegelian dual sense of the term, that is, preserved while transcended. Something of the earlier forms survives in the later ones. Through metamorphosis the core of individuality—*Dämon*, *Monade*, or *Charakter*—would remain intact, yet undergo many changes in the course of the individual's growth. Goethe thus conceived of human individuality as a process analogous to the patterns of development he had observed while engaged in his botanical studies. As Gundolf has pointed out, Goethe was the first German (and given Germany's intellectual preeminence at the time, one may say the first European) to think of human life as a "conscious self-developing," as a "process of self-development achieving consciously what a plant achieves for itself unconsciously."[7] Though Goethe came to regard metamorphosis as the universal principle of change, as the principle effecting the development of animals and man no less than of plants (*GA* 22:803), he considered man the highest incarnation of this natural law of development because in him, once again, the process became aware of itself.

This metamorphic interpretation of human development was Goethe's greatest contribution to the Romantic and, more specifically, to the Emersonian theory of the individual. Through the Goethean idea of metamorphosis, Emerson could preserve both man's continuity with the rest of nature and his uniqueness. Two passages, the first from the essay on "Intellect" and the second from "The Over-Soul," will illustrate how pervasive the metamorphic model was in Emerson's thinking about individual human development:

All our progress is an unfolding, like the vegetable bud. You have first an

6. José Ortega y Gasset, "Concerning a Bicentennial Goethe," 356.
7. Gundolf, *Goethe*, 38.

instinct, then an opinion, then a knowledge, as the plant has root, bud, and fruit. Trust the instinct to the end, though you can render no reason. It is vain to hurry it. By trusting it to the end, it shall ripen into truth, and you shall know why you believe. (*CW* 2:195–96)

The soul's advances are not made by gradation, such as can be represented by motion in a straight line; but rather by ascension of state, such as can be represented by metamorphosis,—from the egg to the worm, from the worm to the fly. (*CW* 2:163)

These passages also show that Emerson has fully understood that meta-morphosis preserves as much as it changes. In a sense, the theory of metamorphosis is but "the philosophical perception of identity through endless mutations of form" (*CW* 2:18).[8]

Important as metamorphosis is, it does not, in Goethe's view, fully account for the development of the individual. The idea of polarity is equally important. One might say that in the growth of the individual, as Goethe imagines it, polarity and metamorphosis continually intersect.

The two polarities that are relevant in this context are both dynamic: true individuality requires a continual accepting and rejecting of either pole. The first polarity, a metaphysical one, comprises the opposites of "Eins und Alles," the One and the All. Either pole, by itself, would destroy individuality, the latter through absorption and the former through isolation. True individuality requires, on the one hand, that we assert our "self" (*uns zu verselbsten*) and, on the other, that we as regularly deny our "self" (*uns zu entselbstigen*) in order to maintain our birthright in the All (*GA* 10:388). Emerson expressed the dynamic tension inherent in this metaphysical polarity through a rich paradox: "self-reliance . . . is reliance on God" (*W* 11:236).

The second polarity, a sociopsychological one, comprises the opposites of the self and its human environment. Surrender to either pole would, again, abolish individuality: the concept "individual" requires the "others" as much as it requires a "self." Three ideas shape Goethe's thinking on the relations between the self and the others: the idea of action, of self-denial, and of reverence. As Goethe sees it, the fundamental relationship between the self and the forces that make up the self's sociocultural environment (e.g., social and political realities, cultural

8. For a general discussion of metamorphosis in Emerson's thought, see Daniel B. Shea, "Emerson and the American Metamorphosis"; and Robert D. Richardson, Jr., *Myth and Literature in the American Renaissance*, 79–83.

heritage, historical "moment," significant contemporaries) is one of interaction. The self achieves individuality through action in and upon the human world and through the world's counteraction. Only through action can the self become aware of the powers of its "daimon" and enhance these powers, and only through action can the self, which is infinite in its aspirations, come to a sense of its limitations (*GA* 9:554, 543). The self becomes aware of its limitations because its actions bring it into conflict with other selves that are also endeavoring to enact their infinite, often very different, aspirations. True individuality arises when the self recognizes the irreducible "otherness" of the others. Like Hegel, Goethe insists that one can be fully an individual only if one grants full individuality to others (*GA* 18:258; 16:912).[9]

Such recognition of the claims of others does not, in Goethe's view, absolve the individual of his duty to be, above all, self-reliant. It would be absurd to claim that Emerson owed his central doctrine of self-reliance to Goethe or to anyone else. What the journals do show is that Emerson eagerly wrote down passages from Goethe and ideas inspired by Goethe that lent support to his high claims for self-reliance:

> "I will no more rest until nothing longer remains to me word and tradition, but lively conception. From youth up, was this my impulse & my torment. . . . " (*JMN* 5:128; *GA* 11:338)

> In the scholar's Ethics, I would put down Beharre wo du stehst. Stick by yourself, and Goethe's practice to publish his book without preface & let it lie unexplained. And further, the sentence in West Ostlichen Divan about *freedom*. (*JMN* 5:187–88; *GA* 9:570; 3:467)

> Goethe . . . makes us prize all our being by suggesting its inexhaustible wealth. (*JMN* 12:189)

> "A strong nature feels itself brought into the world for its own development, & not for the approbation of the public." *Goethe*. (*JMN* 13:105)

Or, as a final example, this statement in support of artistic individuality: "Every description of Man seems at the moment to cover the whole ground & leave no room for future poets. But it is, as Goethe said, 'Twenty great masters have painted the Madonna & Child, but not one can be spared,' & no two interfere" (*JMN* 5:249).

Self-reliance is, of course, one of the hallmarks of genius. The pervasiveness of the *Geniekult* in later eighteenth and earlier nineteenth-

9. Hegel, *Phänomenologie des Geistes*, 139–40.

century thought and literature makes claiming any specific source for Emerson's reflections on the subject extremely hazardous. When Emerson lists definitions of genius in his "Encyclopedia," his authorities include Coleridge, Schelling, Schiller, Richter (Jean Paul), Goethe, Hazlitt, De Staël, Scott, Landor, Charles C. Emerson, and Ralph Waldo Emerson himself (*JMN* 6:195–97, 229). What Goethe does seem to have contributed to Emerson's thinking is, once again, a greater emphasis on the "practical" as opposed to the purely spiritual sources and effects of genius. Emerson quotes two definitions from Goethe in his "Encyclopedia": "What is genius but the faculty of seizing & turning to account every thing that strikes us; of coordinating & breathing life into all the materials that present themselves?" and "Genius is that power of man which by acting & doing gives laws & rules" (*JMN* 6:195–96, *GA* 24:767–68; 10:822). Such a view of genius as dependent upon milieu and action also inspires *Faust, Part Two*, which teaches, among other things, that "the only way for modern man to transform himself . . . is by radically transforming the whole physical and social and moral world he lives in."[10] Emerson often adopts a similarly practical emphasis:

> The popular literary creed seems to be, "I am a sublime genius; I ought not therefore to labor." But genius is the power to labor better and more availably than others. (*CW* 1:211)

> Genius is the activity which repairs the decays of things, whether wholly or partly of a material and finite kind. (*CW* 3:13)

> The true romance which the world exists to realize, will be the transformation of genius into practical power. (*CW* 3:49)

> The secret of genius is . . . first, last, midst, and without end, to honour every truth by use. (*CW* 4:166; final sentence of chapter on Goethe in *Representative Men*)

> Genius is not a lazy angel contemplating itself and things. . . . Thought must take the stupendous step of passing into realization. (*W* 12:43)

The importance which Goethe attaches to action as the daimon's means of attaining the fullness of individuality is further illustrated by his claim that persistent activity provides man with his best hope of immortality. The belief in immortality is far too important to be derived from any legend (*aus einer Legende hernehmen*); it is provable only through the unending pursuit of self-realization: "The entelechy-driven monad [*entelechische Monade*] has but to maintain itself in tireless

10. Berman, *All That is Solid*, 40.

activity; if this activity becomes to it a second nature, it will not lack
work throughout eternity" (*GA* 24:308; 21:728). Emerson repeatedly
echoes Goethe verbally as well as conceptually. In the chapter on "Worship" in *The Conduct of Life* and in a late essay on "Immortality" he
integrates Goethe's idea into his argument with an ease that is evidence
in itself of how Goethean his cast of mind had become in certain
respects. In "Worship" we read that immortality "is a doctrine too great
to rest on any legend. . . . It must be proved, if at all, from our own
activity and designs, which imply an interminable future for their play"
(*W* 6:239). In "Immortality" Emerson quotes Goethe directly: "'To me,'
said Goethe, 'the eternal existence of my soul is proved from my idea of
activity. If I work incessantly till my death, Nature is bound to give me
another form of existence, when the present can no longer sustain my
spirit'" (*W* 8:342; *GA* 24:308). Later in the same essay he echoes
Goethe, insisting, as he did in "Worship," that the belief in immortality
"cannot rest on a legend," but that instead "it must have the assurance of
a man's faculties that they can fill a larger theatre and a longer term than
Nature here allows him" (*W* 8:343–44).

Within the dynamic of the polar tension between "self" and "others,"
man's individuality is shaped not only by action, but also, as already
indicated, by self-denial (*Entsagung*) and reverence (*Ehrfurcht*). Self-
denial involves the recognition that individualism is always based on
exclusions, on selectivity. Such self-imposed exclusions prevent the individual, on the one hand, from growing at the expense of other individuals, and on the other, from falling victim to fragmentation. Goethe's
works contain innumerable passages in praise of the self-imposed re-
strictions necessary to individual wholeness. One of his best-known
statements is the poem "Natur und Kunst," with its insistence on concentration, restriction, and law as prerequisites for achievement (*GA*
2:141). It is entirely in Goethe's spirit that Emerson writes: "The one
prudence in life is concentration; the one evil is dissipation" (*W* 6:73).
Emerson, furthermore, came to recognize that Goethe's self-protective
Entsagung should not be mistaken for selfishness; he concluded that
"Goethe as a man who wished to make the most of himself was right in
avoiding the horrors" (*JMN* 11:188). Emerson must not have found it
too difficult to appreciate Goethe's position on this point since he himself shared to a high degree that tendency toward psychological and
emotional self-protection. Nietzsche exaggerated only slightly when he

said that Emerson was a man "who instinctively fed only on ambrosia and who left alone what was indigestible in things."[11]

Reverence is the subject of a long passage in *Wilhelm Meisters Wanderjahre* that Emerson copied in his journal (*JMN* 6:109–11). Goethe discusses the different kinds of reverence necessary to an attainment of the highest form of individuality. We must revere what is above us, revere what is equal to us, and revere what is below us. "Out of these three reverences arises the highest reverence: reverence for oneself." This highest reverence escapes from presumption and self-conceit only if in its turn it continually vitalizes the other three reverences. Reverence for oneself thus conceived is "the highest attainment of which man is capable"; it allows him, without arrogance, to consider himself "the best that God and nature have produced" (*GA* 8:171–72).

In this same passage Goethe also distinguished between reverence (*Ehrfurcht*) and fear (*Furcht*), especially as they determine religious experience. He rejects any form of religion based on fear because it disunites (*vereint*) the individual from himself (*GA* 8:171). Emerson illustrates this disunity in his attack on the saint as traditionally conceived:

> The saint . . . is a man who accustomed to revere the moral sentiment as a law discriminates it in his thinking from his private self; cuts it off; puts it far from him; calls it by another name; and attributes to himself none of its infinite worthiness; but contrasts the animal tendencies in him, with this overpowering worth; and so, is divided; and calls one, God,—and worships it and calls the other, himself, and flouts it. . . . Whilst the soul eagerly acknowledges the instinct of adoration it not less eagerly rejects a mean, cowering, and dependent attitude, an allegiance to anything external and alien. (*EL* 2:341)

True religion, for Emerson as well as for Goethe, encourages the individual's growth through reverence rather than diminishes him through fear. A conversation with Eckermann shows how Goethe envisioned this growth: "We are made free not by refusing to acknowledge anything above us, but by revering something that is above us. For by revering it, we raise ourselves to its height and show through our recognition that we ourselves have the tendencies of that higher nature in us and are worthy of becoming its equal" (*GA* 24:216–17). This statement also clarifies Goethe's claim that reverence (*Ehrfurcht*) allows a person to keep his honor (*Ehre*) while giving honor (*GA* 8:171). The true beneficiary of reverence, therefore, is not the revered but the reverer—a view which is

---

11. Friedrich Nietzsche, *Gesammelte Werke*, 17:116.

also Emerson's. Defining worship as "the regard for what is above us," Emerson adds: "Men are respectable only as they respect" (*W* 10:205). Summarizing this entire argument about reverence and the self, he declares: "Selfreliance applied to another person is reverence, that is, only the selfrespecting will be reverent" (*JMN* 7:371).

The greatest merit, to Emerson's mind, of Goethe's interpretation of individuality was that it presented the individual as someone in process, in a state of becoming, and thus linked convincingly to nature's development because informed, like nature, by the principles of metamorphosis and polarity. Since, as we have seen, the human individual is the highest product of nature's *Steigerung* (enhancement), Goethe's view also supported Emerson's meliorism and gave it a firm grounding in nature. "*Amelioration in nature,*" Emerson wrote, "alone permits and authorizes amelioration in mankind" (*CW* 1:231). Conceivably, he might have made this claim without inspiration from Goethe. What Goethe did provide, however, was a theory of nature and of man that made such claims respectable in the new world of the nineteenth century. Better than anyone else, Goethe succeeded in reintegrating man and nature without destroying the objective validity of the latter or the freedom and dignity of the former. This accomplishment, perhaps Goethe's greatest, was certainly his most challenging legacy to his century and to ours. Emerson's considerable success in proving himself worthy of that legacy is one reason why he continues to challenge us today.

BIBLIOGRAPHY

Abrams, M. H. *The Mirror and the Lamp: Romantic Theory and the Critical Tradition.* 1953. Reprint. New York: W. W. Norton & Co., 1958.
———. *Natural Supernaturalism: Tradition and Revolution in Romantic Literature.* New York: W. W. Norton & Co., 1971.
Arnold, Matthew. *The Complete Prose Works of Matthew Arnold.* Edited by R. H. Super. 11 vols. Ann Arbor: University of Michigan Press, 1960–1977.
———. *The Poetical Works of Matthew Arnold.* Edited by C. B. Tinker and H. F. Lowry. London: Oxford University Press, 1950.
Ashton, Rosemary. *The German Idea: Four English Writers and the Reception of German Thought, 1800–1860.* Cambridge: Cambridge University Press, 1980.
Bancroft, George. *Literary and Historical Miscellanies.* New York, 1855.
Barzun, Jacques. *Classic, Romantic and Modern.* Garden City, N.Y.: Doubleday & Co., 1961.
Bate, Jonathan. *Shakespeare and the English Romantic Imagination.* Oxford: Clarendon Press, 1986.
Beach, Joseph Warren. *The Concept of Nature in Nineteenth-Century English Poetry.* 1936. Reprint. New York: Russell & Russell, 1966.
Benn, Gottfried. *Gesammelte Werke.* Edited by Dieter Wellershoff. 4 vols. Wiesbaden: Limes Verlag, 1959–1961.
Bercovitch, Sacvan. *The Puritan Origins of the American Self.* New Haven: Yale University Press, 1975.
———, ed. *Typology and Early American Literature.* [Amherst]: University of Massachusetts Press, 1972.
Bergstraesser, Arnold. *Goethe's Image of Man and Society.* Chicago: Henry Regnery Co., 1949.
Berlin, Isaiah. *Vico and Herder: Two Studies in the History of Ideas.* 1976. Reprint. New York: Random House, Vintage Books, 1977.
Berman, Marshall. *All That Is Solid Melts into Air: The Experience of Modernity.* New York: Simon & Schuster, 1982.
Berry, Edmund G. *Emerson's Plutarch.* Cambridge: Harvard University Press, 1961.
Bloom, Harold. *The Anxiety of Influence: A Theory of Poetry.* New York: Oxford University Press, 1973.
———. *The Ringers in the Tower: Studies in Romantic Tradition.* Chicago: University of Chicago Press, 1971.
Bollacher, Martin. *Der junge Goethe und Spinoza.* Tübingen: Max Niemeyer Verlag, 1969.
Boyd, James. *Notes to Goethe's Poems.* 2 vols. Oxford: Basil Blackwell, 1944–1949.
Brann, Henry Athanasius. "Hegel and His New England Echo." In *Critical Es-*

129

says on Ralph Waldo Emerson, edited by Robert E. Burkholder and Joel Myerson, 225–30. Boston: G. K. Hall & Co., 1983.

Buell, Lawrence. *Literary Transcendentalism: Style and Vision in the American Renaissance*. Ithaca: Cornell University Press, 1973.

———. *New England Literary Culture: From Revolution Through Renaissance*. Cambridge: Cambridge University Press, 1986.

———. "The Transcendentalist Movement." In *The Transcendentalists: A Review of Research and Criticism*, edited by Joel Myerson, 1–36. New York: Modern Language Association of America, 1984.

Butler, E. M. *The Tyranny of Greece over Germany*. 1935. Reprint. Boston: Beacon Press, 1958.

Cameron, Kenneth Walter. *Emerson the Essayist*. 2 vols. Raleigh, N.C.: Thistle Press, 1945.

Carlyle, Thomas. *Reminiscences*. Edited by Charles Eliot Norton. 1887. Reprint. London: J. M. Dent & Sons, 1932.

———. *The Works of Thomas Carlyle*. Edited by [Henry Duff Traill]. 30 vols. 1896–1899. Reprint. New York: AMS Press, 1969.

Cascardi, Anthony J. "Emerson on Nature: Philosophy beyond Kant." *ESQ: A Journal of the American Renaissance* 30 (1984): 201–10.

Cassirer, Ernst. *Goethe und die geschichtliche Welt*. Berlin: Verlag Bruno Cassirer, 1932.

———. *Rousseau, Kant and Goethe*. Translated by James Gutmann, Paul Oskar Kristeller, and John Herman Randall, Jr. 1945. Reprint. New York: Harper and Row, 1963.

———. *Wesen und Wirkung des Symbolbegriffs*. Oxford: Bruno Cassirer, 1956.

Chai, Leon. *The Romantic Foundations of the American Renaissance*. Ithaca: Cornell University Press, 1987.

Cirlot, Juan Eduardo. *A Dictionary of Symbols*. Translated by Jack Sage. New York: Philosophical Library, 1962.

Clarke, James Freeman. "Orphic Sayings. From Goethe." *Western Messenger* 2 (1836): 59–62.

———. "Thomas Carlyle." *Western Messenger* 4 (1838): 417–23.

Clarke, James Freeman, Ralph Waldo Emerson, and William Henry Channing, eds. *Memoirs of Margaret Fuller Ossoli*. 2 vols. Boston, 1852.

Collingwood, R. G. *The Idea of Nature*. 1945. Reprint. New York: Oxford University Press, 1960.

Cranch, Christopher Pearse. "Ralph Waldo Emerson." In *Critical Essays on Ralph Waldo Emerson*, edited by Robert E. Burkholder and Joel Myerson, 203–15. Boston: G. K. Hall & Co., 1983.

Curtius, Ernst Robert. *European Literature and the Latin Middle Ages*. Translated by Willard R. Trask. 1953. Reprint. New York: Harper & Row, 1963.

———. "Goethe oder Jaspers?" (1949). In *Goethe im Urteil seiner Kritiker*, edited by Karl Robert Mandelkow, 4:304–07. Munich: Verlag C. H. Beck, 1984.

Dictionnaire biographique des auteurs (Laffont-Bompiani). 2 vols. Paris: Société d'Édition des Dictionnaires et Encyclopédies, 1964.

Dihle, Albrecht. *Studien zur griechischen Biographie*. Göttingen: Vandenhoeck & Ruprecht, 1956.

Donoghue, Denis. "Emerson at First: A Commentary on *Nature*." In *Emerson and His Legacy: Essays in Honor of Quentin Anderson*, edited by Stephen Donadio, Stephen Railton, and Ormond Seavey, 23–47. Carbondale: Southern Illinois University Press, 1986.

Eichhorn, Peter. *Idee und Erfahrung im Spätwerk Goethes*. Freiburg: Verlag Karl Alber, 1971.

Eichner, Hans. "The Rise of Modern Science and the Genesis of Romanticism." *PMLA* 97 (1982): 8–30.

Eliot, T. S. *On Poetry and Poets*. New York: Farrar, Straus & Giroux, 1961.

———. *The Use of Poetry and the Use of Criticism*. 1933. Reprint. London: Faber & Faber, 1964.

Ellison, Julie. *Emerson's Romantic Style*. Princeton: Princeton University Press, 1984.

"Emerson's Essays." *The United States Magazine and Democratic Review* 16 (1845): 589–602.

Emrich, Wilhelm. *Die Symbolik von "Faust II."* Frankfurt am Main: Athenäum Verlag, 1964.

Everett, Edward. *Orations and Speeches, on Various Occasions*. 1836. Reprint. New York: Arno Press, 1972.

Fairley, Barker. *A Study of Goethe*. 1947. Reprint. Westport, Conn: Greenwood Press, 1977.

Feidelson, Charles, Jr. *Symbolism and American Literature*. Chicago: University of Chicago Press, 1953.

Fichte, Johann Gottlieb. *Sämmtliche Werke*. 8 vols. 1845–1846. Reprint. Berlin: Walter de Gruyter & Co., 1965.

Frost, Robert. "On Emerson." In *Emerson: A Collection of Critical Essays*, edited by Milton R. Konvitz and Stephen E. Whicher, 12–17. Englewood Cliffs, N.J.: Prentice-Hall, 1962.

Frothingham, Octavius Brooks. *Transcendentalism in New England: A History*. 1876. Reprint. New York: Harper & Brothers, 1959.

Gadamer, Hans-Georg. *Wahrheit und Methode: Grundzüge einer philosophischen Hermeneutik*. 3d ed. Tübingen: J. C. B. Mohr, 1972.

Goddard, Harold Clarke. *Studies in New England Transcendentalism*. 1908. Reprint. New York: Hillary House, 1960.

Gundolf, Friedrich. *Goethe*. Berlin: Georg Bondi, 1916.

Hartman, Geoffrey H. *Criticism in the Wilderness: The Study of Literature Today*. New Haven: Yale University Press, 1980.

Haskins, David Greene. *Ralph Waldo Emerson: His Maternal Ancestors, With Some Reminiscences of Him*. Boston, 1886.

Hegel, Georg Wilhelm Friedrich. *Phänomenologie des Geistes*. Edited by Johannes Hoffmeister. Hamburg: Verlag von Felix Meiner, 1952.

———. *Sämtliche Werke*. Edited by Hermann Glockner. 20 vols. 1927–1930. Reprint. Stuttgart: Friedrich Frommann Verlag, 1956–1965.

Hopkins, Vivian C. "The Influence of Goethe on Emerson's Aesthetic Theory." *Philological Quarterly* 27 (1948): 325–44.

———. *Spires of Form: A Study of Emerson's Aesthetic Theory*. 1951. Reprint. New York: Russell & Russell, 1965.

Houghton, Walter E. *The Victorian Frame of Mind, 1830–1870*. New Haven: Yale University Press, 1957.

Hyppolite, Jean. *Genèse et structure de la "Phénoménologie de l'esprit" de Hegel*. Paris: Aubier-Montaigne, 1946.

James, Henry. "Emerson." In *The American Essays of Henry James*, edited by Leon Edel, 51–76. New York: Vintage Books, 1956.

James, William. *The Varieties of Religious Experience*. 1902. Reprint. London: Longmans, 1929.

Jaspers, Karl. "Unsere Zukunft und Goethe" (1947). In *Aneignung und Polemik*, 121–41. Munich: R. Piper & Co. Verlag, 1968.

Jeffrey, Francis. "German Genius and Taste: Goethe's *Wilhelm Meister*." *Edinburgh Review* 42 (1825). Reprint. *Contributions to the "Edinburgh Review*," by Francis Jeffrey, 104–20. New York, 1866.

Korff, Hermann August. *Geist der Goethezeit*. 5 vols. 1923–1957. Reprint. Leipzig: Koehler & Amelang, 1964–1966.

Kroner, Richard. *Von Kant bis Hegel*. 2 vols. 1921–1924. Reprint. Tübingen: J. C. B. Mohr, 1977.

Kronick, Joseph G. *American Poetics of History: From Emerson to the Moderns*. Baton Rouge: Louisiana State University Press, 1984.

Kurtz, Kenneth. "The Sources and Development of Emerson's *Representative Men*." Ph.D. diss., Yale University, 1947.

Lewes, George Henry. *The Life and Works of Goethe*. 1855. Reprint. London: J. M. Dent & Sons, 1908.

Lukács, Georg. *Faust und Faustus: Vom Drama der Menschengattung zur Tragödie der modernen Kunst*. Reinbek bei Hamburg: Rowohlt, 1967.

———. *The Historical Novel*. Translated by Hannah and Stanley Mitchell. London: Merlin Press, 1962.

McCormick, John O. "Emerson's Theory of Human Greatness." *New England Quarterly* 26 (1953): 291–314.

McFarland, Thomas. *Coleridge and the Pantheist Tradition*. Oxford: Clarendon Press, 1969.

———. *Originality & Imagination*. Baltimore: Johns Hopkins University Press, 1985.

———. *Romanticism and the Forms of Ruin: Wordsworth, Coleridge, and Modalities of Fragmentation*. Princeton: Princeton University Press, 1981.

MacRae, Donald. "Emerson and the Arts." *The Art Bulletin* 20 (1938): 78–95.

Mandelkow, Karl Robert. *Goethe in Deutschland*. 1 vol. to date. Munich: Verlag C. H. Beck, 1980–.

Mann, Thomas. *Gesammelte Werke*. 12 vols. [Frankfurt am Main]: S. Fischer Verlag, 1960.

Marache, Maurice. *Le Symbole dans la pensée et l'oeuvre de Goethe*. Paris: A. G. Nizet, 1960.

Martini, Fritz. *Deutsche Literaturgeschichte: Von den Anfängen bis zur Gegenwart*. 7th ed. Stuttgart: Alfred Kröner Verlag, 1955.

———. "Modern, Die Moderne." In *Reallexikon der deutschen Literaturgeschichte*, edited by Werner Kohlschmidt et al., 2d ed., 2:391–415. Berlin: Walter de Gruyter & Co., 1964.

Matthiessen, F. O. *American Renaissance: Art and Expression in the Age of Emerson and Whitman*. New York: Oxford University Press, 1941.

Meinecke, Friedrich. *Die Entstehung des Historismus*. Munich: R. Oldenbourg Verlag, 1965.

Meyer, Hans. "Der Weg zur Geschichte: *Dichtung und Wahrheit*." In *Goethe: Ein Versuch über den Erfolg*, 108–33. Frankfurt am Main: Suhrkamp Verlag, 1973.

Meyer-Abich, Adolf. *Die Vollendung der Morphologie Goethes durch Alexander von Humboldt*. Göttingen: Vandenhoeck & Ruprecht, 1970.

Miller, Perry. "Emersonian Genius and the American Democracy." *New England Quarterly* 26 (1953): 27–44.

———. "From Edwards to Emerson." In *Errand into the Wilderness*, 184–203. 1956. Reprint. New York: Harper & Row, 1964.

Mott, Frank Luther. *A History of American Magazines*. 5 vols. Cambridge: Harvard University Press, 1930–1968.

Nietzsche, Friedrich. *Gesammelte Werke*. 23 vols. Munich: Musarion Verlag, 1920–1929.

Novalis [Friedrich von Hardenberg]. *Schriften*. Edited by Paul Kluckhohn and Richard Samuel. 4 vols. Stuttgart: Verlag W. Kohlhammer, 1960–1975.

Ortega y Gasset, José. "Concerning a Bicentennial Goethe." In *Goethe and the Modern Age*, edited by Arnold Bergstraesser, 349–62. Chicago: Henry Regnery Co., 1950.

Patterson, Mark. "Emerson, Napoleon, and the Concept of the Representative." *ESQ: A Journal of the American Renaissance* 31 (1985): 230–42.

Pochmann, Henry A. *German Culture in America: Philosophical and Literary Influences, 1600–1900*. Madison: University of Wisconsin Press, 1957.

Poirier, Richard. "Human, All Too Inhuman." *The New Republic*, 2 February 1987, 29–36.

———. *The Renewal of Literature: Emersonian Reflections*. New York: Random House, 1987.

Porte, Joel. "Emerson, Thoreau, and the Double Consciousness." *New England Quarterly* 41 (1968): 40–50.

———. *Representative Man: Ralph Waldo Emerson in His Time*. New York: Oxford University Press, 1979.

Porter, David. *Emerson and Literary Change*. Cambridge: Harvard University Press, 1978.

Praz, Mario. *The Hero in Eclipse in Victorian Fiction*. Translated by Angus Davidson. London: Oxford University Press, 1956.

"Quarterly List of New Publications." *North American Review* 51 (1840): 521–30.

Richardson, Robert D., Jr. "Emerson's Italian Journey." *Browning Institute Studies* 12 (1984): 121–31.

———. *Myth and Literature in the American Renaissance*. Bloomington: Indiana University Press, 1978.

Robinson, David. *Apostle of Culture: Emerson as Preacher and Lecturer*. Philadelphia: University of Pennsylvania Press, 1982.

Rusk, Ralph L. *The Life of Ralph Waldo Emerson*. New York: Charles Scribner's Sons, 1949.

Sakmann, Paul. *Ralph Waldo Emerson's Geisteswelt*. Stuttgart: Friedrich Frommann Verlag, 1927.

Schiller, Friedrich. *Werke*. Edited by Herbert Kraft et al. 4 vols. Frankfurt am Main: Insel Verlag, 1966.

Schlegel, Friedrich. *Athenäum*, Fragment 216. In *Kritische Friedrich-Schlegel-Ausgabe*, edited by Ernst Behler et al., 2:198–99. Munich: Verlag Ferdinand Schöningh, 1967.

———. Letter to August Wilhelm Schlegel, 27 February 1794. Quoted in Peter Szondi, *Poetik und Geschichtsphilosophie*, 1:115. Frankfurt am Main: Suhrkamp Verlag, 1974.

Schmitz, Hermann. *Goethes Altersdenken im problemgeschichtlichen Zusammenhang*. Bonn: H. Bouvier & Co. Verlag, 1959.

Schuler, Reinhard. *Das Exemplarische bei Goethe: Die biographische Skizze zwischen 1803 und 1809*. Munich: Wilhelm Fink Verlag, 1973.

Schwinger, Reinhold. "Innere Form." In Reinhold Schwinger and Heinz Nicolai, *Innere Form und dichterische Phantasie*, 1–89. Munich: C. H. Beck'sche Verlagsbuchhandlung, 1935.

[Sears, Barnas]. "German Literature;—Its Religious Character and Influence." *The Christian Review* 6 (1841): 269–84.

Shea, Daniel B. "Emerson and the American Metamorphosis." In *Emerson: Prophecy, Metamorphosis, and Influence*, edited by David Levin, 29–56. New York: Columbia University Press, 1975.

Simmel, Georg. *Goethe*. Leipzig: Klinkhardt & Biermann, 1913.

Slater, Joseph. "Goethe, Carlyle, and the Open Secret." *Anglia* 76 (1958): 422–26.

Staiger, Emil. *Goethe*. 3 vols. Zurich: Atlantis Verlag, 1952–1959.

Stange, G. Robert. *Matthew Arnold: The Poet as Humanist*. Princeton: Princeton University Press, 1967.

Stein, Philipp, ed. *Goethe-Briefe*. 8 vols. Berlin: Wertbuchhandel, 1924.

Steinbrink, Jeffrey. "Novels of Circumstance and Novels of Character: Emerson's

View of Fiction." *ESQ: A Journal of the American Renaissance* 20 (1974): 101–10.

Strauch, Carl F. "The Year of Emerson's Poetic Maturity: 1834." *Philological Quarterly* 34 (1955): 353–77.

Strich, Fritz. *Goethe und die Weltliteratur*. 2d ed. Bern: Francke Verlag, 1957.

Super, R. H. *The Time-Spirit of Matthew Arnold*. Ann Arbor: University of Michigan Press, 1970.

Tocqueville, Alexis de. *Democracy in America*. Translated by Henry Reeve, revised by Francis Bowen, edited by Phillips Bradley. 2 vols. New York: Alfred A. Knopf, 1945.

Todorov, Tzvetan. *Theories of the Symbol*. Translated by Catherine Porter. Ithaca: Cornell University Press, 1982.

Trilling, Lionel. *Beyond Culture*. New York: Viking Press, 1968.

———. *The Opposing Self*. New York: Viking Press, 1955.

Trunz, Erich, ed. *Goethe-Gedichte*. Munich: Verlag C. H. Beck, 1974.

Van Cromphout, Gustaaf. "Emerson and the Dialectics of History." *PMLA* 91 (1976): 54–65.

Viëtor, Karl. *Goethes Anschauung vom Menschen*. Bern: Francke Verlag, 1960.

———. *Goethe the Poet*. Translated by Moses Hadas. Cambridge: Harvard University Press, 1949.

———. *Goethe the Thinker*. Translated by Bayard Q. Morgan. Cambridge: Harvard University Press, 1950.

Vogel, Stanley M. *German Literary Influences on the American Transcendentalists*. 1955. Reprint. [Hamden, Conn.]: Archon Books, 1970.

Wahr, Frederick B. *Emerson and Goethe*. Ann Arbor: George Wahr, 1915.

Walser, Martin. "Things Go Better With Goethe." *The New York Times Book Review*, 2 March 1986.

Weintraub, Karl Joachim. *The Value of the Individual: Self and Circumstance in Autobiography*. Chicago: University of Chicago Press, 1978.

Wellek, René. *Concepts of Criticism*. New Haven: Yale University Press, 1963.

———. *Confrontations: Studies in the Intellectual and Literary Relations between Germany, England, and the United States during the Nineteenth Century*. Princeton: Princeton University Press, 1965.

———. *Discriminations: Further Concepts of Criticism*. New Haven: Yale University Press, 1970.

———. *A History of Modern Criticism, 1750–1950*. 6 vols. to date. New Haven: Yale University Press, 1955–.

Wertheim, Ursula. "Zu Problemen von Biographie und Autobiographie in Goethes Ästhetik." In *Goethe-Studien*, 89–126. Berlin: Rütten & Loening, 1968.

Whicher, Stephen E. *Freedom and Fate: An Inner Life of Ralph Waldo Emerson*. 1953. Reprint. New York: A. S. Barnes & Co., 1961.

Whitaker, Thomas R. "The Riddle of Emerson's 'Sphinx,'" *American Literature* 27 (1955): 179–95.

Willoughby, Leonard A. "The Living Goethe." In Elizabeth M. Wilkinson and Leonard A. Willoughby, *Goethe: Poet and Thinker*, 9–19. London: Edward Arnold, 1970.

———. "Unity and Continuity in Goethe." In Elizabeth M. Wilkinson and Leonard A. Willoughby, *Goethe: Poet and Thinker*, 214–28. London: Edward Arnold, 1970.

Wimsatt, William K., Jr., and Cleanth Brooks. *Literary Criticism: A Short History*. New York: Alfred A. Knopf, 1957.

Wyman, Mary A. *The Lure for Feeling in the Creative Process*. New York: Philosophical Library, 1960.

Yoder, R. A. *Emerson and the Orphic Poet in America*. Berkeley: University of California Press, 1978.

INDEX